What people are saying

"Here at Citibank we use the Quick Course® computer training book series for 'just-in-time' job aids—the books are great for users who are too busy for tutorials and training. Quick Course® books provide very clear instruction and easy reference."

Bill Moreno, Development Manager
Citibank
San Francisco, CA

"At Geometric Results, much of our work is PC related and we need training tools that can quickly and effectively improve the PC skills of our people. Early this year we began using your materials in our internal PC training curriculum and the results have been outstanding. Both participants and instructors like the books and the measured learning outcomes have been very favorable."

Roger Hill, Instructional Systems Designer
Geometric Results Incorporated
Southfield, MI

"The concise and well organized text features numbered instructions, screen shots, and useful quick reference pointers, and tips…[This] affordable text is very helpful for educators who wish to build proficiency."

Computer Literacy column
Curriculum Administrator Magazine
Stamford, CT

"I have purchased five other books on this subject that I've probably paid more than $60 for, and your [Quick Course®] book taught me more than those five books combined!"

Emory Majors
Searcy, AR

"I would like you to know how much I enjoy the Quick Course® books I have received from you. The directions are clear and easy to follow with attention paid to every detail of the particular lesson."

Betty Weinkauf, Retired Senior
Mission, TX

QUICK COURSE®

in

MICROSOFT®

EXCEL 97

ONLINE PRESS INC. •

Microsoft Press

PUBLISHED BY
Microsoft Press
A Division of Microsoft Corporation
One Microsoft Way
Redmond, WA 98052-6399

Library of Congress Cataloging-in-Publication Data

Quick Course in Microsoft Excel 97 / Online Press Inc.
      p.   cm.
   Includes index.
   ISBN 1-57231-723-X
   1. Microsoft Excel for Windows. 2. Business- -Computer programs.
   3. Electronic spreadsheets.   I. Online Press Inc.
   HF5548.4.M523Q53   1997
   005.369- -dc21   97-27391
                                              CIP

Printed and bound in the United States of America.

3 4 5 6 7 8 9   WCWC   2 1 0 9

Distributed in Canada by ITP Nelson, a division of Thomson Canada Limited.

A CIP record of this book is available from the British Library.

Microsoft Press books are available through booksellers and distributors worldwide. For further information about international editions, contact your local Microsoft Corporation office. Or contact Microsoft Press International directly at fax (425) 936-7329. Visit our Web site at mspress.microsoft.com.

A Quick Course® Education/Training Edition for this title is published by Online Press Inc. For information about supplementary workbooks, contact Online Press Inc. at 14320 NE 21st St., Suite 18, Bellevue, WA, 98007, USA, 1-800-854-3344.

Authors: Joyce Cox, Polly Urban, and Christina Dudley of Online Press Inc., Bellevue, Washington
Acquisitions Editor: Susanne M. Forderer
Project Editor: Maureen Williams Zimmerman

From the publisher

"I love these books!"

I can't tell you the number of times people have said those exact words to me about our new Quick Course® software training book series. And when I ask them what makes the books so special, this is what they say:

- **They're short and approachable, but they give you hours worth of good information.**

  Written for busy people with limited time, most Quick Course books are designed to be completed in 15 to 40 hours. Because Quick Course books are usually divided into two parts—Learning the Basics and Building Proficiency—users can selectively choose the chapters that meet their needs and complete them as time allows.

- **They're relevant and fun, and they assume you're no dummy.**

  Written in an easy-to-follow, step-by-step format, Quick Course books offer streamlined instruction for the new user in the form of no-nonsense, to-the-point tutorials and learning exercises. Each book provides a logical sequence of instructions for creating useful business documents—the same documents people use on the job. People can either follow along directly or substitute their own information and customize the documents. After finishing a book, users have a valuable "library" of documents they can continually recycle and update with new information.

- **They're direct and to the point, and they're a lot more than just pretty pictures.**

  Training-oriented rather than feature-oriented, Quick Course books don't cover the things you don't really need to know to do useful work. They offer easy-to-follow, step-by-step instructions; lots of screen shots for checking work in progress; quick-reference pointers for fast, easy lookup and review; and useful tips offering additional information on topics being discussed.

- **They're a rolled-into-one-book solution, and they meet a variety of training needs.**

  Designed with instructional flexibility in mind, Quick Course books can be used both for self-training and as the basis for weeklong courses, two-day seminars, and all-day workshops. They can be adapted to meet a variety of training needs, including classroom instruction, take-away practice exercises, and self-paced learning.

Microsoft Press is very excited about bringing you this extraordinary series. But you must be the judge. I hope you'll give these books a try. And maybe the next time I see you, you too will say, "Hey, Jim! I love these books!"

Jim Brown, Publisher
Microsoft Press

Content overview

PART ONE: LEARNING THE BASICS

1 Getting Started

To learn the basics of Excel, we build a simple table for tracking sales by invoice. We show you how to get information into Excel, and how to save and retrieve files.

2 Editing and Formatting Worksheets

In this chapter, we show you how to edit worksheets and check spelling. We then cover some formatting basics and complete the chapter with a discussion of printing.

3 Performing Calculations

Here, you learn how to build formulas to perform calculations on your data. We introduce you to Excel's functions, including the decision-making IF function, and we finish up by consolidating data.

PART TWO: BUILDING PROFICIENCY

4 Visually Presenting Data

Excel's sophisticated autoformats and graphing capabilities help you analyze a budget by displaying its components visually. We create a graph on the worksheet and then format it in a variety of ways.

5 Extracting Information from a List

In Excel, a list is a simple database. Our examples show how to sort data and use powerful yet efficient tools to extract and manipulate information. We also create a pivot table and summarize data.

6 More Advanced Calculations

We build a set of worksheets and link them so that formulas in one worksheet can look up information in another. Then we cover three types of what-if analysis: goal-seeking, data tables, and scenarios.

Index

Content details

3 Performing Calculations   58

PART TWO: BUILDING PROFICIENCY

6 More Advanced Calculations   134

PART ONE

LEARNING THE BASICS

In Part One, we cover basic techniques for working with Microsoft Excel. After you have completed these three chapters, you will know enough to be able to handle the majority of spreadsheets you will create with Excel. In Chapter 1, you learn how to work with the program while creating a simple sales log on Sheet1 of a workbook. In Chapter 2, you edit and format the worksheet, find out more about workbooks, and learn how to print. Finally, in Chapter 3, you use some of Excel's built-in functions to quickly create formulas that enable you to perform calculations.

1

Getting Started

To learn the basics of Excel, we build a simple table for tracking sales by invoice. We show you how to get information into Excel by entering different types of data, how to give Excel instructions, and how to save and retrieve files.

Date	Product Name	Customer Number	Amount of Sale
3-Jan-97	Kiwi Spree	4739AA	1456.23
4-Jan-97	Midnite Espresso	943200	875.56
10-Jan-97	Rootbeer Float	1488AA	2068.3
24-Jan-97	Just Peachy	6398AA	1399.07
2-Feb-97	Oh Fudge!	7945AA	2643.9
8-Feb-97	P B & J	825600	10576.4
14-Feb-97	Kiwi Spree	246500	345.23
1-Mar-97	Thanks a Latte	5409AA	1168.34
11-Mar-97	P B & J	3867AA	2256.23
15-Mar-97	Midnite Espresso	975600	656.9
20-Mar-97	Just Peachy	479300	345
28-Mar-97	Oh Fudge!	6563AA	2531.76

At first glance, Microsoft Excel 97 can seem pretty intimidating, especially if you've never worked with a spreadsheet program before. But like most software programs, Excel loses its scary aura if you take the time to learn it in easily digestible chunks. In this chapter, we discuss some jargon and then cover how to enter text and numbers, move around a worksheet, give instructions, save files, and get help. After we discuss these fundamentals, you'll easily be able to follow along with the examples in the rest of the book.

We assume that you've already installed Windows 95 and Microsoft Excel 97 on your computer. We also assume that you've worked with Windows 95 before and that you know how to start programs, move windows, choose commands from menus, highlight text, and so on. If you are a Windows novice, we suggest that you take a look at *Quick Course in Windows 95*, another book in the Quick Course series, which will help you quickly come up to speed. Well, enough preamble, let's get going:

Starting Excel

1. Choose Programs and then Microsoft Excel from the Windows 95 Start menu.

2. If necessary, close the Office Assistant by clicking the Start Using Microsoft Excel option (we discuss the Office Assistant on page 22). Your screen now looks like the one shown at the top of the facing page.

Other ways to start Excel

Instead of starting Excel by choosing it from the Start menu, you can create a shortcut icon for Excel on your Windows 95 desktop. Right-click an open area of the desktop and choose New and then Shortcut from the object menu. In the Create Shortcut dialog box, click the Browse button, navigate to Program Files\Microsoft Office\Excel.exe, and click Next. Then type a name for the shortcut icon and click Finish. (To delete a shortcut icon, simply drag it to the Recycle Bin.) For maximum efficiency, you can start Excel and open an existing document by choosing Documents from the Start menu and then choosing the document from the Documents submenu, where Windows 95 stores the names of up to 15 of the most recently opened files. If you are using Microsoft Office, you can click the Open Office Document button on the Office shortcut bar and navigate to the folder in which the document you want to open is stored, or you can choose Open Office Document from the top of the Start menu. To start Excel and open a new document, click the New Office Document button on the Office shortcut bar or choose New Office Document from the top of the Start menu.

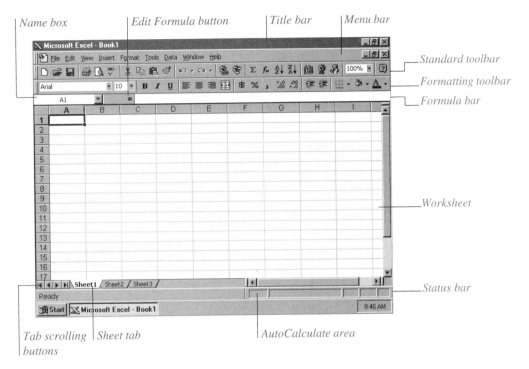

Name box   Edit Formula button   Title bar   Menu bar

Standard toolbar
Formatting toolbar
Formula bar

Worksheet

Status bar

Tab scrolling   Sheet tab   AutoCalculate area
buttons

Taking up the majority of the screen is a *blank worksheet*, which, as you can see, is laid out in a grid of *columns* and *rows* like the ledger paper used by accountants. There are 256 columns, lettered A through IV, and 65,536 rows, numbered 1 through 65536. The rectangle at the junction of each column and row is called a *cell*. To identify each of the 16 million plus cells on the worksheet, Excel uses an *address*, or *reference*, that consists of the letter at the top of the cell's column and the number at the left end of its row. For example, the reference of the cell in the top left corner of the worksheet is A1. The *active cell*—the one we're working with—is designated on the worksheet by a heavy border. Excel displays the reference of the active cell in the *name box* at the left end of the formula bar.

Cell addresses

The *status bar* at the bottom of the window includes an *AutoCalculate area*, where Excel displays the sum of the entries in the selected cells. For more information about the AutoCalculate area, see page 72.

An Overview of Workbooks

The worksheet on your screen is just one sheet in the current file, which is called a *workbook*. By default, each new workbook contains 3 sheets. However, a single workbook file can contain as many as 255 sheets, named Sheet1 through Sheet255. We can have several types of sheets in one workbook, including worksheets, chart sheets (where we create graphs of worksheet data), and macro sheets (where we store automated ways of manipulating data). This workbook format allows us to store related data on separate sheets but in a single file. (The topic of macros is too advanced for this book, but if you're interested, you can read about macros in Excel's online Help. See page 22 for information about how to use Help.)

Sheet tabs

For each sheet in a workbook, Excel displays a *tab*, like a file-folder tab, above the status bar at the bottom of the screen. These tabs are handy for moving from sheet to sheet. Try this:

Displaying sheets

1. Click the Sheet2 tab. Excel displays that sheet.

2. Next, click the Sheet3 tab to display that sheet and finish by selecting Sheet1.

Entering Data

Most worksheets consist of tables of numbers, called *values* in spreadsheet jargon, on which we perform various calculations using equations, which are called *formulas*. We can also enter *dates*, *times*, and *text*. (Dates and times are considered values because we can use them in calculations; see the tip on page 12.) In this section, we'll get the ball rolling by entering some text, values, and dates in a simple worksheet for an ice cream company called *Cream of the Crop*. We'll see how to enter formulas in Chapter 3.

As you'll see in the next section, you can complete the entries you make in the worksheet's cells in several different ways. For convenience, we've summarized these ways at the top of the facing page.

The tab scrolling buttons

The number of sheets in the workbook may exceed the number of tabs Excel can display at the bottom of the worksheet window. You can use the tab scrolling buttons to the left of the Sheet1 tab to bring the tabs for hidden sheets into view, without changing the active sheet. Click the First Sheet or Last Sheet button to display the tabs for those sheets and the Previous Sheet or Next Sheet button to move tabs into view one at a time.

To do this...	Use this...
Stay in the same cell	Enter button
Move down	Enter key or Down Arrow
Move up	Shift+Enter or Up Arrow
Move right	Tab key or Right Arrow
Move left	Shift+Tab or Left Arrow

Entering Text

To make our worksheets easy to read, we usually enter text as column and row headings that describe the associated entries. Let's try entering a few headings now:

1. With cell A1 selected, type *Date*. As you type, the text appears in both the cell and the formula bar, and a blinking insertion point in the cell tells you where the next character you type will be inserted. A Cancel button (✗) and an Enter button (✓) appear between the text and name box. Meanwhile, the indicator in the status bar changes from Ready to Enter because the text you have typed will not be recorded in cell A1 until you "enter" it.

Entering headings

2. Click the Enter button to complete the entry. Excel enters the Date heading in cell A1, and the indicator changes to Ready. The entry is left-aligned in its cell. (Unless you tell Excel to do otherwise, it always left-aligns text.)

3. Click cell B1 to select it. The reference displayed in the name box changes from A1 to B1.

4. Type *Product Name*, but instead of clicking the Enter button to enter the heading in the cell, press the Tab key. Excel completes the entry in cell B1 and selects cell C1.

5. Type *Customer Number* and press the Tab key.

6. Now enter one more heading. In cell D1, type *Amount of Sale* and click the Enter button to complete the entry. Turn the page to see how the newly entered row of headings looks in the worksheet.

Changing what the Enter key does

If you prefer that the Enter key moves your selection in a direction other than down, you can adjust it. To do so, choose Options from the Tools menu and click the Edit tab. In the Move Selection After Enter setting, click the arrow next to the Direction edit box and click OK.

Long text entries

Notice that the headings in cells B1, C1, and D1 are too long to fit in their cells. Until we entered the Customer Number heading in cell C1, the Product Name heading spilled over into C1, just as Amount of Sale spills over from D1 into E1. After we entered the Customer Number heading, Excel truncated Product Name so that we could read the heading in C1. The Product Name and Customer Number headings are still intact, however. (If you're skeptical, click either cell and look at the formula bar.) After we have entered more information, we'll adjust the column widths to accommodate long entries (see page 18).

That completes the column headings. Now let's turn our attention to the rest of the table. We'll skip the Date column for now and enter the names of a few ice-cream flavors in column B:

Correcting mistakes

If you make a mistake, you can click the cell containing the error and simply type the new entry. If you want to correct part of an entry, click its cell and press F2, or double-click the cell, so that you can edit the entry directly in the cell. You can then press Home or End to move the insertion point to the beginning or end of the entry and press Right Arrow or Left Arrow to move the insertion point forward or backward one character. Press Backspace to delete the character before the insertion point or Delete to delete the character after the insertion point. Then type the correction and click the Enter button.

1. Click cell B2 and type *Kiwi Spree*.

2. Instead of clicking the Enter button, press the Enter key. Excel completes the entry in B2 and selects B3.

3. In cell B3, type *Midnite Espresso* and press the Enter key to complete the entry and move to cell B4.

4. Next type the following names in the Product Name column, pressing the Enter key after each one:

   B4   *Rootbeer Float*
   B5   *Just Peachy*
   B6   *Oh Fudge!*

5. In cell B7, type *P*. Excel anticipates that you'll type *Product Name*. When you type the first characters of a repeated text entry in the same column, Excel's AutoComplete feature finishes the entry for you. If Excel's entry is correct, you can

move on to the next entry; but since it's not, complete the entry by typing a space and then *B & J* and pressing Enter.

6. Continue with the following entries, simply pressing Enter when Excel's entry is correct:

B8	*Kiwi Spree*
B9	*Thanks a Latte*
B10	*P B & J*
B11	*Midnite Espresso*
B12	*Just Peachy*
B13	*Oh Fudge!*

Entering Numbers as Text

Now let's enter the customer numbers in column C. Normally, we want Excel to treat customer numbers—and social security numbers, part numbers, phone numbers, and other numbers that are used primarily for identification—as text rather than as values on which we might want to perform calculations. If the "number" includes not only the digits 0 through 9 but also letters and other characters (such as hyphens), Excel usually recognizes it as text. However, if the number consists of only digits and we want Excel to treat it as text, we have to explicitly tell Excel to do so.

For demonstration purposes, assume that the Cream of the Crop company sells ice cream to both large chain stores and individually-owned ("mom and pop") stores. All stores are denoted by a customer number with six characters. The customer numbers for large chain stores consist of four digits followed by the letters AA, and the customer numbers for individually-owned stores consist of six digits that end with 00 (two zeros). Follow these steps to see how Excel treats these customer numbers:

1. Click cell C2, type *4739AA,* and press the Enter key. This customer number consists of both digits and letters, so Excel treats the entry as text and left-aligns it.

2. In cell C3, which is now active, type *943200* and click the Enter button. This customer number consists of only digits, so Excel treats the entry as a value and right-aligns it.

Pick From List

You don't have to type repeated text entries in a column. You can right-click the next cell in the column and choose Pick From List from the object menu to display a drop-down list of the entries you've already typed. You can then select the next entry from the list rather than typing it.

How do we tell Excel to treat an entry that consists of only digits as text? We begin the entry with an apostrophe ('). Follow these steps:

1. In cell C3, type '943200 *and press Enter. (When you type the new entry, Excel overwrites the old entry.) Because of the apostrophe, Excel recognizes the new entry as text.

2. Enter the customer numbers shown below in the indicated cells, preceding those that end in 00 with an apostrophe so that Excel will treat them as text:

C4	*1488AA*
C5	*6398AA*
C6	*7945AA*
C7	*'825600*
C8	*'246500*
C9	*5409AA*
C10	*3867AA*
C11	*'975600*
C12	*'479300*
C13	*6563AA*

Here are the results:

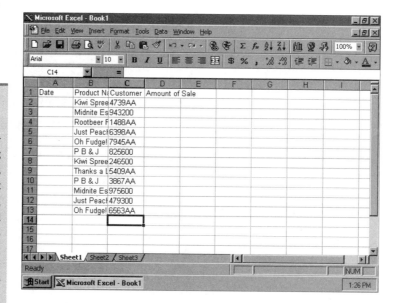

Formatting numbers as text

You can make Excel treat an existing value as text by selecting the cell containing the value, choosing Cells from the Format menu, and on the Number tab, selecting the Text format and clicking OK. You can format values as Zip codes, phone numbers, and social security numbers by selecting Special on the Number tab and then selecting the appropriate Type option.

Entering Values

As you have seen, entering numeric values is just as easy as entering text. Follow along with the next two steps as we enter the sales amounts in column D:

1. Click cell D2 to select the first cell in the Amount of Sale column, and type *1456.23*. Press Enter to complete the entry, which Excel right-aligns in its cell.

2. Type the following amounts in the indicated cells, pressing Enter after each one:

   D3   *875.56*
   D4   *2068.30*
   D5   *1399.07*
   D6   *2643.90*
   D7   *10576.40*
   D8   *345.23*
   D9   *1168.34*
   D10   *2256.23*
   D11   *656.90*
   D12   *345.00*
   D13   *2531.76*

Don't worry if Excel does not display these values exactly as you entered them. Unless we tell it otherwise, Excel displays values in their simplest form. On page 48, we tell Excel to display the values as dollars and cents, and then the missing zeros will reappear.

Entering Dates and Times

For a date or time to be displayed correctly, we must enter it in a format that Excel recognizes as a date or time. Excel then displays the entry as we want it but stores it as a value so that we can perform date and time arithmetic (see the tip on page 12). The following formats are recognized:

3/4	4-Mar-97	March 4, 1997
3/4/97	04-Mar-97	M
03/04/97	Mar-97	M-97
4-Mar	March-97	

Long numeric values

Excel allows a long text entry to overflow into an adjacent empty cell and truncates the entry only if the adjacent cell also contains an entry. However, Excel treats a long numeric value differently. If Excel displays pound signs (#) instead of the value you entered, the value is too large to display in the cell. By default, values are displayed in scientific notation, and values with many decimal places might be rounded. For example, if you enter 12345678912345 in a standard width cell (a standard width cell holds 8.43 characters, but Excel estimates the width for long numeric values and adjusts the column accordingly), Excel displays 1.23457E+13 (1.23457 times 10 to the 13th power). And if you enter 123456.789 in a standard width cell, Excel displays 123456.8. In both cases, Excel leaves the underlying value unchanged, and you can widen the column to display the value in the format in which you entered it. Note that if you then apply formatting changes to the numeric value, Excel automatically widens the column so that the value is fully displayed. (Adjusting the width of columns is discussed on pages 18 and 43.)

Two additional formats combine both date and time and take these forms:

3/4/97 1:30 PM   3/4/97 13:30

Let's see how Excel handles different date formats:

1. Type the dates shown here in the indicated cells, pressing the Enter key after each one:

A2	*Jan 3, 1997*
A3	*1/4/97*
A4	*1/10/97*
A5	*24-Jan-97*
A6	*Feb 2, 97*
A7	*2/8/97*
A8	*feb 14, 97*
A9	*3/1/97*
A10	*11-March-97*
A11	*3-15-97*
A12	*3/20/97*
A13	*March 28, 1997*

Again, don't worry if Excel displays the dates differently from the way you entered them. Later, we'll come back and make sure all the dates appear in the same format. As you can see here, we've now completed all the columns of this simple worksheet:

Date and time arithmetic

Each date you enter is internally recorded by Excel as a value that represents the number of days that have elapsed between that date and the base date of January 1, 1900, which is assigned the value 1. As a result, you can perform arithmetic with dates—for example, you can have Excel determine whether a payment is past due. Similarly, when you enter a time, it is internally recorded as a decimal value that represents the portion of the day that has elapsed between that time and the base time of 12:00 midnight.

Moving Around

The fastest way to move around the worksheet is with the mouse. As you've seen, clicking any cell moves the cell pointer to that location and displays a new reference in the name box at the left end of the formula bar. To display parts of the worksheet that are currently out of sight, you can use the scroll bars, which function the same way as scroll bars in all Windows applications. Try this:

1. With cell A1 selected, click the arrows at the bottom of the vertical scroll bar and the right end of the horizontal scroll bar until cell P37 comes into view.

   Using the scroll bars

2. Drag the scroll box in the vertical scroll bar. As you drag, Excel displays the number of the screen's topmost row. If you drag the horizontal scroll box, Excel displays the letter of the screen's leftmost column.

3. Press Ctrl+Home to jump back to cell A1.

   Jumping to cell A1

As we just demonstrated, you can use the keyboard to move around the worksheet. You'll probably use the four arrow keys most often, but as you gain more experience with Excel, you might find other keys and key combinations useful for moving around by more than one cell at a time. Here is a list of some of the navigation keys and what they do:

Jumping to a specific cell

To do this...	Use this...
Scroll down one window length	Page Down
Scroll up one window length	Page Up
Scroll right one window width	Alt+Page Down
Scroll left one window width	Alt+Page Up
Move to end of active area	Ctrl+End
Move to cell A1	Ctrl+Home
Move to first cell in row containing active cell	Home
Move to last cell in row containing active cell	End, then Right Arrow
Move to first cell in column containing active cell	End, then Up Arrow
Move to last cell in column containing active cell	End, then Down Arrow

The Go To command

Another way to move around the worksheet is with the Go To command. Choose Go To from the Edit menu to display the Go To dialog box. Type the address of the cell you want to move to in the Reference edit box and click OK. Immediately, Excel scrolls the worksheet and selects that cell.

Selecting Ranges

Well, we've created a basic worksheet. But before we can show you some of the things you can do with it, we first need to discuss how to select blocks of cells, called *ranges*. Any rectangular block or blocks containing more than one cell is a range. A range can include two cells, an entire row or column, or the entire worksheet. *Range references* consist of the address of the cell in the top left corner of the rectangular block and the address of the cell in the bottom right corner, separated by a colon. For example, A1:B2 identifies the range that consists of cells A1, A2, B1, and B2.

Selecting and working with ranges saves us time because we can apply formats to or reference the whole range, instead of dealing with each cell individually. The simplest way to learn how to select ranges is to actually do it, so follow these steps:

Ranges →

Range references →

Selecting with the mouse →

1. Point to cell A1, hold down the left mouse button, and drag diagonally to cell D13 without releasing the button. Notice as you drag that the reference in the name box at the left end of the formula bar reads 13R x 4C, which indicates that you are selecting a range of cells 13 rows high by 4 columns wide.

2. Release the mouse button when the range A1:D13 is high-lighted. As you can see here, cell A1—the cell where you started the selection—is white, indicating that it is the active cell in the range:

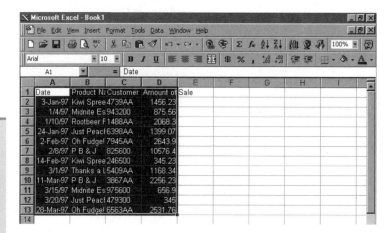

Selecting more than one block

A range can consist of more than one block of cells. To select a multiblock range, select the first range, hold down the Ctrl key, select the next range, and so on.

3. Press Ctrl+Home to move to cell A1, and then click column
   B's *header*—the gray box at the top of the column containing
   the letter *B*—to select the entire column. (You can select an
   entire row by clicking its header—the gray box on the left
   containing the row number.)

Selecting entire columns
and rows

Next, try selecting ranges with the keyboard:

1. Select cell B6, hold down the Shift key, press the Right Arrow
   key twice and the Down Arrow key twice, and release the
   Shift key. The range B6:D8 is selected.

Selecting with the keyboard

2. Click anywhere on the worksheet to deselect the range.

Giving Excel Instructions

Now that we know how to select cells and ranges, let's quickly
cover how we tell Excel what it should do with the selection.

Using Menus

We can give Excel instructions by choosing *commands* that
are arranged in *menus* on the menu bar. Because this procedure is the same for all Windows applications, we assume that
you are familiar with it and provide only a quick review here.
If you are a new Windows user, we suggest that you spend a
little time becoming familiar with the mechanics of menus,
commands, and dialog boxes before proceeding.

To choose a command from a menu, we first click the menu
name on the menu bar. When the menu drops down, we
simply click the name of the command we want. To do the
same thing with the keyboard, we can press the Alt key to
activate the menu bar, press the underlined letter of the name
of the menu, and then press the underlined letter of the
command we want.

Choosing commands

Some command names are followed by an arrowhead, indicating that a *submenu* will appear when we choose that
command. We choose commands from submenus as we
would from regular menus.

Submenus

Dialog boxes

Some command names are followed by an ellipsis (...), indicating that we must supply more information before Excel can carry out the command. When we choose one of these commands, Excel displays a *dialog box*. Some dialog boxes have several sheets called *tabs*. We can display the options on a tab by clicking it. We give the information needed to carry out a command by typing in an *edit box* or by selecting options from *lists* and clicking *check boxes* and *option buttons*. We close the dialog box and carry out the command according to our specifications by clicking a command button—usually OK or Close—or by clicking the Close button in the top right corner. Clicking Cancel closes the dialog box and cancels the command. Other command buttons might be available to open other dialog boxes or to refine the original command.

Some command names are occasionally displayed in gray letters, indicating that we can't choose those commands. For example, the Paste command on the Edit menu appears in gray until we have used the Cut or Copy command.

As a short example of how to use menu commands and dialog boxes, follow these steps to apply a display format to the dates we entered in column A of the worksheet:

1. Use the mouse or keyboard to select the range A2:A13, which contains the dates.

2. Click Format on the menu bar to drop down the Format menu.

3. Click the Cells command to display this dialog box:

Menu command buttons

You may have noticed that on certain menu commands, an icon appears to the left of the command name. This simply indicates that a corresponding button exists for this command on one of Excel's toolbars.

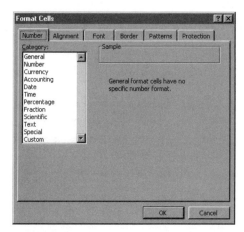

The Format Cells dialog box contains six tabs for formatting different aspects of a cell, allowing you to handle all the formatting from this one dialog box. The first tab—Number—should be displayed. If it isn't, click it.

4. Click Date in the Category list.

5. Click 04-Mar-97 in the Type list. Then click OK to close the dialog box and apply the format to the selected cells.

6. Press Ctrl+Home to move to cell A1. Excel displays all the dates in the same format, as shown here:

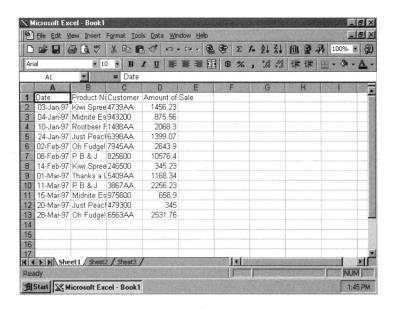

If a value is too long for its cell, Excel fills the cell with pound signs. (See the tip on page 11.) To see the actual value, we must widen the column containing the cell. We quickly look at one technique for widening columns on the next page. For more detailed information, see page 43.

Help with dialog boxes

In the top right corner of most dialog boxes is a question mark button that provides information about the dialog box, including how to complete its edit boxes and select its options. To use the question mark button, click it once and then click an item in the dialog box. A pop-up window appears, containing information about the item.

Using Object Menus

Object menus are context-sensitive menus that group together the commands used frequently with a specific type of object, such as a cell or a window element. We display the object menu by pointing to the object and clicking the right mouse button. (From now on, we will refer to this action as *right-clicking*.) We can then choose a command from the menu in the usual way. Try this:

Right-clicking

1. Point to column B's header (the gray box containing the letter *B*), and click the left mouse button to select the entire column.

2. Right-click the selection to display this object menu:

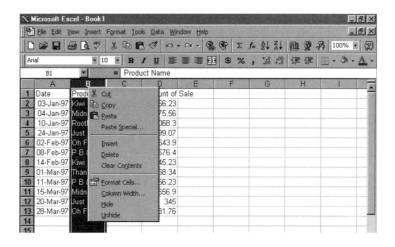

Widening columns

3. Choose Column Width from the menu to display this dialog box, where Excel has entered the column's current width:

4. In the Column Width edit box, type *16* and press Enter (the equivalent of clicking OK). Excel almost doubles the width of the cells in the selected column, where all the entries are now completely visible.

5. Select columns C and D by pointing to C's header, holding down the left mouse button, dragging across D's header, and releasing the button. Then repeat steps 2 through 4 to widen these two columns simultaneously.

In this book, we use object menus whenever they are the most efficient method of giving Excel instructions.

Using Toolbars

Another way to give instructions is by clicking buttons on a toolbar. Excel comes with many built-in toolbars: some that you will use frequently and others you may never use. By default, Excel displays only the Standard and Formatting toolbars, but we can display a different toolbar at any time (see page 97). We can also move, resize, and hide the toolbars. Throughout this book we use toolbar buttons whenever possible because they are often the fastest way to access commands. Let's do some exploring:

1. Point to any button on the Standard toolbar. Excel's *ToolTips* feature displays a box with the button's name.

ToolTips

2. Move the pointer slowly over each button and box on the Standard and Formatting toolbars so that ToolTips displays its name.

3. Click the Web Toolbar button on the Standard toolbar to display the Web toolbar shown here:

The Web Toolbar button

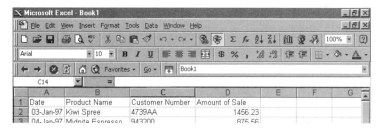

If the Web toolbar is already turned on, clicking the Web Toolbar button turns it off. This type of button is called a *toggle*, because it toggles a specific feature, in this case the Web toolbar, on and off. If necessary, click the Web Toolbar button again to turn on the toolbar.

The Web toolbar

If you have a modem and are connected to the Internet, you can easily browse Web pages through Excel using the Web toolbar. For more information, choose Contents And Index from the Help menu and on the Contents tab, select a topic under Using Microsoft Excel With The Internet, Your Intranet, Or A Local Web.

4. Use ToolTips to get an idea of what you can do with this toolbar and read the tip below for more information about using the Web with Excel. When you're finished, click the Web Toolbar button again to remove the toolbar.

Displaying toolbars ⟶ 5. Now right-click anywhere on the Standard or Formatting toolbar to display an object menu that lists some of the other available toolbars, as shown here:

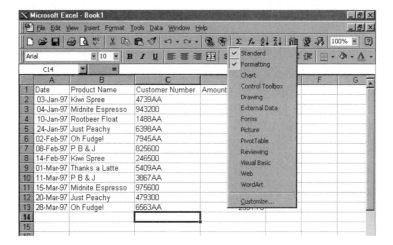

6. Choose Chart from the object menu to display a floating Chart toolbar.

7. Double-click the toolbar's title bar to move it to the toolbar area above the worksheet window, as shown below:

8. Point to the double line on the left side of the Chart toolbar and drag it from the toolbar area over the worksheet.

9. Click the Close button at the right end of the toolbar's title bar to remove the toolbar from the screen.

Using Keyboard Shortcuts

If you and your mouse don't get along and you prefer to use the keyboard, you can access many Excel commands with keyboard shortcuts. You can display lists of these shortcuts by choosing the Contents And Index command from the Help menu, double-clicking Reference Information on the Contents tab, double-clicking Keyboard Shortcut Reference, and then double-clicking the keyboard shortcut topic you're interested in. (For more information about Excel's Help system, see page 22.)

Saving Workbooks

Let's save the workbook we are working with for future use. As you'll see if you follow these steps, the first time we save a workbook, we must give its file a name:

1. Click the Save button on the Standard toolbar. Because you have not yet assigned a name to the workbook, Excel displays the Save As dialog box shown on the next page.

The Save button

Save options

Clicking the Options button in the Save As dialog box displays the Save Options dialog box. Selecting the Always Create Backup option prompts Excel to create a copy of the existing version of the workbook before overwriting it with the new version. Excel gives the copy the name Backup of *Filename*. Assigning a password in the Protection Password To Open edit box tells Excel not to open the workbook until the password is entered correctly. Assigning a password in the Password To Modify edit box tells Excel to open a read-only version of the workbook if the password is not entered correctly. The read-only version can be altered but can be saved only with a different name. Selecting the Read-Only Recommended option tells Excel to warn users that the workbook should be opened as read-only, but does not prevent opening the workbook in the usual way. Other save options are available on the General tab of the dialog box that appears when you choose Options from the Tools menu. For example, you can specify a default directory for your workbooks in the Default File Location edit box.

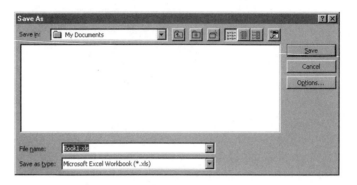

2. Excel suggests *Book1* as the name for the first workbook created during this Excel session. This name is not very descriptive, so with *Book1* highlighted in the File Name edit box, type *1997 Sales*.

3. Be sure the My Documents folder appears in the Save In box and, leaving the other settings in the dialog box as they are, click Save. When you return to the worksheet, notice that the name 1997 Sales has replaced Book1 in the title bar.

Saving existing workbooks

Preserving the previous version

From now on, we can save this workbook by simply clicking the Save button. Excel then saves the workbook by overwriting the previous version with a new version. If we want to save the changes we have made to a workbook but preserve the previous version, we can assign the new version a different name by choosing the Save As command from the File menu, entering a new filename, and clicking Save.

Getting Help

Are you worried that you might not remember everything we've covered so far? Don't be. If we forget how to carry out a particular task, help is never far away. You have already seen how the ToolTips feature can jog your memory about the functions of the toolbar buttons. Here we'll look at ways to get information using the Office Assistant, a new feature of Excel 97, which you've probably seen pop up a few times already:

The Office Assistant button

1. Click the Office Assistant button on the Standard toolbar. The Office Assistant appears, asking what you would like to do, in a box like this one:

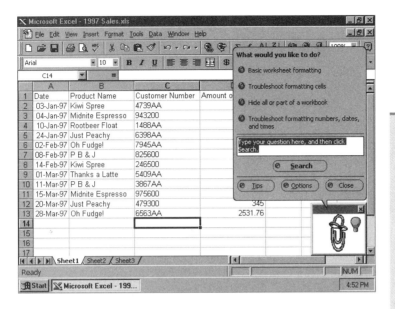

2. Type *How do I save?* in the Search box and then click the Search button to have the Office Assistant search for topics that most closely match your question. The Office Assistant displays another pop-up box:

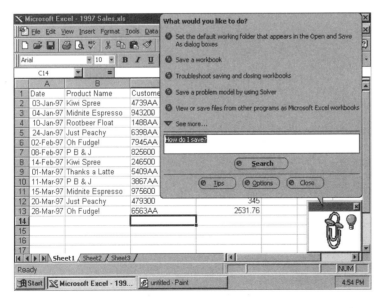

3. Click the Save A Workbook option to display a Help window with the requested information. (It may take a few seconds for the Help file to be prepared for viewing.)

More about the Office Assistant

If the Office Assistant button displays a light bulb, the Office Assistant has a tip for you. Click the button and then click the light bulb in the Office Assistant box to see the tip. If you want to leave the Office Asssistant open, you can move it by dragging its title bar, and you can size it by dragging its frame (only two sizes are available). You can then display the search box by clicking the title bar. If having the Office Assistant on the screen bothers you, or if you would like to customize it, click the Office Assistant's Options button to open the Office Assistant dialog box. Here, you can select and deselect various options that control when the Office Assistant appears, whether it makes sounds, and what tips it displays. If you want the Office Assistant to appear only when you click the Office Assistant button on the Standard toolbar, deselect the Respond To F1 Key, Help With Wizards, and Display Alerts options in the Assistant Capabilities section on the Options tab. On the Gallery tab, you can click the Next button to scroll through the different animated choices for the assistant (the default is the paper clip) and then click OK to change the assistant. (You will need to insert your Office CD-ROM to complete the switch.)

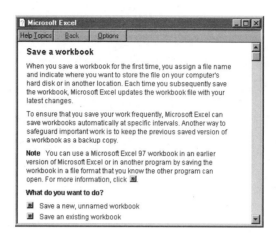

4. Click the arrow to the left of the Save An Existing Workbook option to display instructions on how to complete the task.

5. Click the Close button (the one with the X) to close the Help window and then click the Office Assistant's Close button.

If you prefer to access online Help without the aid of the Office Assistant, you can simply use the Help menu. Follow these steps:

Using the Help Index →

1. Choose Contents And Index from the Help menu and click the Index tab to display this dialog box:

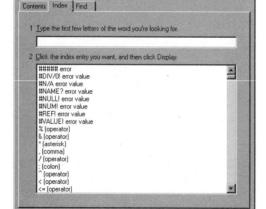

Using the Web for help

If you have a modem and are connected to the Internet, you can quickly access Microsoft's Web site to get help or technical support. Simply choose Microsoft On The Web from the Help menu to display a submenu, and then choose the appropriate option.

2. In the edit box, type *saving* and then click the Display button. In the Topics Found box, click Save A Workbook and then click the Display button to see the Help window shown on the facing page.

3. Click the arrow to the left of Save A Copy Of A Workbook... to display instructions as before. (Note that you can click the Show Me button to open the Save As dialog box without closing the Help window.)

4. Read through the instructions and then close the window.

We'll leave you to explore other Help topics on your own.

Quitting Excel

Well, that's it for the basic tour. All that's left is to show you how to end an Excel session. Follow these steps:

1. Choose Exit from the File menu.

2. If Excel asks whether you want to save the changes you have made to the open worksheet, click Yes.

Here are some other ways to quit Excel:

- Click the Close button at the right end of Excel's title bar.

- Press Alt, then F, and then X.

- Double-click the Control menu icon—the X next to the words *Microsoft Excel*—at the left end of Excel's title bar.

2

Editing and Formatting Worksheets

In this chapter, we show you how to edit worksheets and check spelling. We then demonstrate techniques for editing workbooks. Next, we cover some formatting basics and then complete the chapter with a discussion of printing.

Dress up titles and subtitles by varying the font and size

Set custom headers and footers

1997 Sales.xls

Preliminary Sales Analysis

1st Quarter, 1997

Date	Product Name	Customer Number		Amount of Sale
1/3/97	Kiwi Spree	4739AA		$ 1,456.23
1/4/97	Midnight Espresso	943200		$ 875.56
1/10/97	Rootbeer Float	1488AA		$ 2,068.30
1/24/97	Just Peachy	6398AA		$ 1,399.07
2/2/97	Oh Fudge!	7945AA		$ 2,643.90
2/8/97	P B & J	825600		$ 1,057.64
2/14/97	Kiwi Spree	246500		$ 345.23
3/1/97	Thanks a Latte	5409AA		$ 1,168.34
3/11/97	P B & J	3867AA		$ 2,256.23
3/15/97	Midnight Espresso	975600		$ 656.90
3/20/97	Just Peachy	479300		$ 345.00
3/28/97	Oh Fudge!	6563AA		$ 2,531.76

Page 1

Make headings bold and centered

Copy styles with the click of a button

Check the spelling of text entries

Insert entire columns or rows

Use a currency format to display values as dollars and cents

There are many tasks we might want to perform with a worksheet, and as long as the worksheet is accurate, it will do its job well enough. So our first priority is making sure that the worksheet is set up properly. When we know that the content of the worksheet is correct, we can turn our attention to the way the worksheet looks and focus on making its information easy to decipher.

In this chapter, we first cover the editing techniques that enable us to produce accurate information, and then we take a look at simple formatting techniques that enhance the information's readability.

Opening Existing Workbooks

When we first start Excel, the workbook window contains a blank document named Book1. We can open a workbook we have already created using several methods. If the workbook is one of the last four we have worked with, we can simply choose the file from the bottom of the File menu. Otherwise, we can use the Open button on the Standard toolbar or the Open command on the File menu to retrieve the workbook. We'll use the second method:

The Open button

1. If necessary, start Excel, and then click the Open button on the Standard toolbar to display this dialog box:

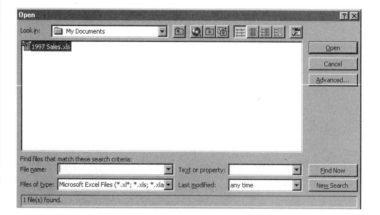

File management

With Excel 97, you can delete, rename, or move your files from Excel's Open or Save As dialog box. For example, by right-clicking a filename in the Open dialog box, you can choose from several object-menu commands that allow you to print the file, send a copy of it to a floppy disk, fax or e-mail a copy of it, delete it, or rename it. In addition, you can save a file in a folder that doesn't yet exist by clicking the Create New Folder button in the Save As dialog box and creating the folder as part of the save operation.

2. Excel should display the contents of your My Documents folder (the folder displayed when you last saved or opened a workbook). If it doesn't, click the arrow to the right of the Look In box and navigate through the folders on your hard drive until you can select the My Documents folder from the drop-down list.

3. If 1997 Sales is already selected, click the Open button to open the workbook. If it is not already selected, double-click it to simultaneously select and open it.

Editing Basics

While creating the 1997 Sales workbook in Chapter 1, you may have corrected the odd typo or two by backspacing over errors and retyping entries correctly. We can take care of most simple edits this way. But for more complicated changes, we can use a variety of more sophisticated editing techniques, as you'll see when you follow the examples in this section.

Changing Entries

First let's cover how to change individual entries. Glancing at the Amount of Sale column in Sheet1 of the 1997 Sales workbook, notice that the amount in cell D7 is suspiciously large compared with all the other amounts. Suppose we check this number and find to our disappointment that the amount should be 1057.64, not 10576.40. To correct the entry without having to retype the whole thing, follow these steps:

1. Double-click cell D7 to select the cell and position an insertion point in the current entry.

2. Point between the 7 and 6 in the cell and click the left mouse button to reposition the insertion point. Then type a period.

3. Click between the second period and the 4 and press the Backspace key to delete the second period.

4. Press Enter to confirm the corrected entry.

   You can also click a cell and press F2 to edit its entry.

Finding workbooks

At the bottom of the Open dialog box are boxes that provide an easy way of locating the file you need. Suppose you can't remember exactly what you called the 1997 Sales workbook or where you stored it. Simply navigate to the folder for your C: drive, click the New Search button, enter *1997 Sales* in the File Name edit box, and click the Commands And Settings button at the top of the dialog box. Choose Search Subfolders from the drop-down menu to tell Excel to look in all the folders on your C: drive. Excel searches the specified drive and its subfolders for any Excel workbooks with the words *1997 Sales* in the filename and displays the ones it finds. You can then select the workbook you want and click the Open button. If you have many workbooks with similar names, you can refine the search by specifying text included in the document or its date of modification, or you can click the Advanced button and specify additional criteria. You can also save searches in the Advanced Find dialog box.

Copying Entries

We can copy an entry or group of entries anywhere within the same worksheet or in a different worksheet. Copy operations involve the use of two buttons: Copy and Paste. We can click these buttons on the Standard toolbar, or we can choose the equivalent commands from the Edit menu. Follow these steps:

The Copy button

The Paste button

1. Select A1:D13 and click the Copy button or choose Copy from the Edit menu. Excel stores a copy of the entries in the selected range on the *Clipboard* (see the tip below).

2. Select cell E1 and click the Paste button or choose Paste from the Edit menu. Excel assumes that the selected cell is the top left corner of the paste area and pastes the copied entries into E1:H13. Notice that you don't have to select the entire paste area. Also notice that Excel does not transfer the column-width settings of the copied cells to the paste area.

Now try using Excel's object menus:

1. Select cell F1 and then right-click to display this object menu:

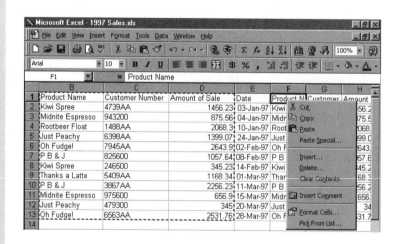

2. Choose Paste from the object menu. Excel uses the selected cell as the top left corner of the paste area and, without warning, pastes the copied cells over the existing contents of cells F1:I13, as shown on the facing page.

The Clipboard

The Clipboard temporarily stores cut or copied data from all Windows applications. You can use it to transfer data from one file to another in the same application or from one application to another. Each item you cut or copy overwrites the previous item. Because the Clipboard is a temporary storage place, turning off your computer erases any information stored there. To preserve information from one session to the next, you can save the contents of the Clipboard as a file by first choosing Programs from the Windows Start menu and choosing ClipBook Viewer from the Accessories submenu. If the contents of the Clipboard are not displayed, choose Clipboard from the ClipBook Viewer's Window menu. Then choose Save As from the File menu, assign the file a name, and click OK.

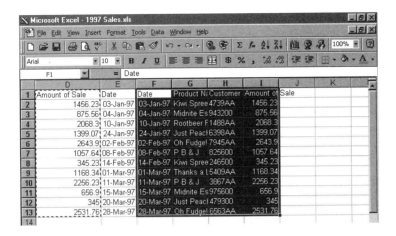

Cause for panic? Not at all. Excel's Undo command is designed for just such an occasion.

3. Click the Undo button or choose Undo Paste from the Edit menu. Excel restores your worksheet to its prepaste status.

The Undo button

Up to now, we have been working with Sheet1 of the 1997 Sales workbook, but suppose we need to set up a second worksheet with a structure similar to that of Sheet1. Do we have to enter all the information again? No; we can copy between worksheets, or even between workbooks, as easily as within one worksheet. The information we just copied is still on the Clipboard, so let's make a copy of it in Sheet2:

1. Click the Sheet2 tab to display that sheet.

2. With cell A1 selected, click the Paste button. Excel faithfully pastes in a copy of the range from Sheet1.

We can also use a simple mouse operation called AutoFill to copy and paste cells. Follow these steps:

1. With A1:D13 selected in Sheet2, move the pointer to the tiny square—called the *fill handle*—in bottom right corner of the selected range.

2. When the pointer changes to a black cross, hold down the left mouse button and drag to the right until the outline of the selection is over the range E1:H13. (Notice as you drag that Excel displays the heading of the column it will copy.)

Undoing and redoing multiple actions

In Excel, you can undo and redo several actions at a time. Simply click the arrow to the right of the appropriate button and then drag through the actions in the list that you want to undo or redo. You cannot undo or redo a single action other than the last one you performed. For example, to undo the third action in the list, you must also undo the first and second actions.

3. Release the mouse button. Excel fills the outline with a copy of the selected cells.

4. Click the Sheet1 tab to return to Sheet1, and press Ctrl+Home.

The result of dragging the fill handle is similar to using the Copy and Paste buttons or the equivalent commands, except that Excel doesn't place a copy of the selected range on the Clipboard.

Moving Entries

When working with two different worksheets in the same workbook, it is sometimes easier to display each worksheet in a separate window. We can use the New Window command to display the current workbook in a second window. The windows are distinguished by numbers displayed in their title bars, after the workbook name. In the following example, we first display 1997 Sales in a second window, and then we'll move entries from one part of the worksheet in one window to another part of the worksheet in the other window. Let's get going:

Displaying a second window

1. Choose the New Window command from the Window menu. Excel displays a copy of the workbook in the new window and names the window 1997 Sales:2.

2. Click Window on the menu bar to drop down its menu, and notice that the names of the two windows appear at the bottom of the menu. Click 1997 Sales:1 to display it.

Copying and moving with the keyboard

You can use keyboard shortcuts to copy a range to the Clipboard and then paste it from the Clipboard into your worksheet. Select the range and press Ctrl+C. Then click the cell in the top left corner of the destination range and press Ctrl+V. To move the range instead of copying it, follow the same procedure but use Ctrl+X instead of Ctrl+C.

3. To show both windows on the screen at the same time, choose Arrange from the Window menu to display this dialog box:

4. Click OK to accept the default Tiled option. Your window now looks like this:

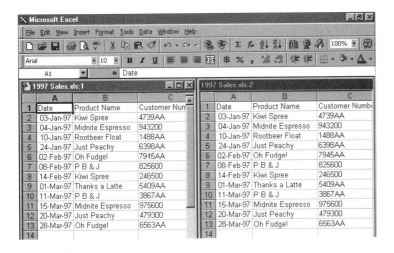

The procedure for moving cell entries is almost identical to that for copying entries. Again, we use two buttons: Cut and Paste. We can click these buttons on the Standard toolbar, or we can choose the equivalent commands from the Edit menu.

5. In 1997 Sales:1, scroll columns E through H into view. Then select E1:H13 and click the Cut button.

The Cut button

6. Activate 1997 Sales:2 by clicking its title bar and then click Sheet2's tab to display Sheet2.

7. Scroll to cell I1 in Sheet2, select it, and click the Paste button. Excel moves the entries from Sheet1 of 1997 Sales:1 to Sheet2 of 1997 Sales:2. The worksheets now look like this:

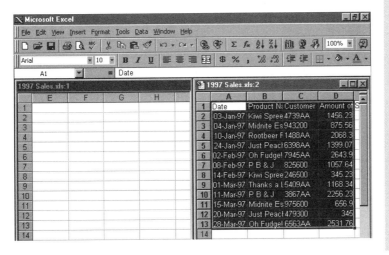

Other window arrangements

In addition to the Tiled option, which arranges windows like tiles on a counter, the Arrange Windows dialog box offers three other configurations. Selecting the Horizontal option allocates an equal amount of horizontal space to each open window, whereas selecting Vertical allocates an equal amount of vertical space. Selecting Cascade arranges the windows so that they overlap in a fan, with the title bar of each one visible. To arrange only the windows of the current workbook, select the Windows Of Active Workbook option.

We can also move entries by dragging them with the mouse and "dropping" them in their new location. Here's how *drag-and-drop editing* works:

Drag-and-drop editing

The Next Sheet button

1. In 1997 Sales.xls:2, check the Next Sheet button to the left of the sheet tabs to display Sheet3's tab without deselecting I1:L13 in Sheet2.

2. Point to the bottom border of the selected range in Sheet2, and when the pointer changes to a hollow arrow, hold down the Alt key and the left mouse button and drag the outline of the selection to the Sheet3 tab (don't release the key or the mouse button yet). Sheet3 opens.

3. While still holding down the left mouse button and the Alt key, drag the outline of the selection over the range A1:D13. Then release the mouse button and the Alt key. Excel moves the selected entries from Sheet2 to their new location in Sheet3.

4. Now display the Sheet3 tab of 1997 Sales:1, which contains the same information as Sheet3 of 1997 Sales:2 because the same workbook is open in both windows. (Later in this chapter, we will work with different workbooks open in two windows; see page 40.)

We can also copy rather than move entries between worksheets using drag-and-drop editing. Just hold down Ctrl+Alt and the left mouse button while dragging.

Now that we're finished moving data between sheets, we can close the second window:

Closing windows

1. Close the 1997 Sales:2 window by first clicking its title bar to activate it and then clicking its Close button.

Maximizing windows

2. Next maximize the 1997 Sales window by clicking its Maximize button—the middle of the three buttons at the right end of the title bar.

The Previous Sheet button

3. Finally, display Sheet1 by clicking the Previous Sheet button to the left of the sheet tabs and then clicking its tab.

Inserting and Deleting Cells

It is a rare person who can create a worksheet from scratch without ever having to tinker with its design—moving this block of data, changing that heading, or adding or deleting a column here and there. In this section, we'll show you how to insert and delete cells. Follow these steps:

1. Press Ctrl+Home to move to cell A1.

2. Click the column D header—the box containing the letter *D*—to select the entire column.

3. Right-click the column and choose Insert from the object menu. Excel inserts an entire blank column in front of the Amount of Sale column which is now column E:

Inserting a row works exactly the same way as inserting a column. We simply click the row header—the box containing the row number—to select the entire row and choose Insert from the row's object menu or Rows from the Insert menu.

Inserting rows

What if we need to insert only a few cells and inserting an entire column or row will mess up some of our entries? We can insert cells anywhere we need them, as you'll see by following these steps:

1. Select E1:E10—all but three of the cells containing entries in column E—and choose Cells from the Insert menu. Excel displays the dialog box shown on the next page.

Inserting cells

Because you have selected a range rather than an entire column or row, Excel needs to know how to move the existing cells to make room for the inserted cells.

2. Click OK to accept the default option of shifting cells to the right. Excel inserts a new blank cell to the left of each selected cell, as shown here:

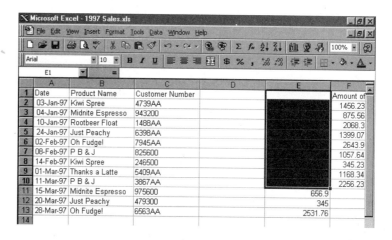

We could undo this insertion to restore the integrity of the Amount of Sale column, but instead let's delete E1:E10:

Deleting cells →

1. With E1:E10 selected, choose Delete from the Edit menu. Excel displays a Delete dialog box similar to the Insert dialog box shown above.

2. Click OK to accept the default option of shifting cells to the left to fill the gap created by the deleted cells. Excel deletes the cells, and the sale amounts are now back in one column.

Leave the empty column D where it is for now—we'll use it when we work with the 1997 Sales workbook again in the next chapter.

Clearing Cells

Clearing cells is different from cutting entries. Cutting entries assumes that we will paste the entries somewhere else, whereas clearing cells simply erases the entries. In the following example, we'll clear some cells on Sheet3 and Sheet2:

1. Click the Sheet3 tab and select A1:D13.

2. Choose Clear from the Edit menu. Excel displays the submenu shown here:

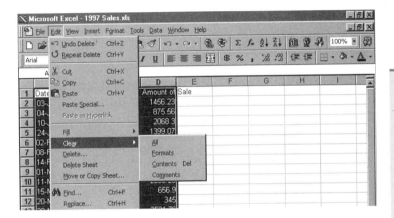

The All option clears all formats, contents, and comments from the cells. Formats clears only the formats, and Contents clears only the contents. Comments clears any attached comments (see the tip on page 42), leaving the formats and contents intact.

3. Choose All. The entries in the range disappear.

4. Display Sheet2 and clear A1:H13 by pressing the Delete key. Excel clears the contents of the cells. (When you press the Delete key, Excel leaves any formats and comments intact.)

5. Return to Sheet1 by clicking the Sheet1 tab.

Checking Spelling

At the end of this chapter, we'll print Sheet1 of the 1997 Sales workbook, but because we will usually want to spell check our worksheets before we print them, we'll pause here to discuss Excel's spell checker. We can check all or part of a

AutoCorrect

Excel's AutoCorrect feature corrects simple typos as you enter text in a worksheet. For example, if you type *teh*, AutoCorrect automatically replaces it with *the*. By default, AutoCorrect also corrects two initial capital letters, such as *EXcel*, and capitalizes the names of days. To include your own commonly misspelled entries in AutoCorrect, choose AutoCorrect from the Tools menu and when the AutoCorrect dialog box appears, type the misspelling in the Replace edit box and the correct spelling in the With edit box, and then click Add. AutoCorrect adds the new entry to its list of common misspellings. (You might want to peruse this list to get a feel for the kinds of words AutoCorrect fixes by default.) You can also delete any entries in AutoCorrect's list by selecting the entry and clicking the Delete button. To turn the AutoCorrect feature off, select the Replace Text As You Type option in the AutoCorrect dialog box.

worksheet for misspelled words and duplicate words within a block. From the Spelling dialog box, we can also add words to one of the dictionaries Excel uses to check our work (see the tip below). Let's run a spell check to see how the spell checker works:

1. Press Ctrl+Home to move to cell A1.

The Spelling button

2. Click the Spelling button. Excel starts checking the worksheet, stops on *Midnite*, and displays this dialog box:

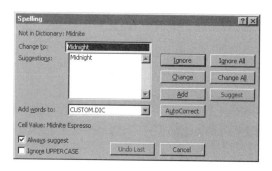

Excel's dictionaries

Excel checks your spelling by first comparing each word in a worksheet to those in its built-in dictionary and the Custom.dic supplemental dictionary. If it finds a word that is not in either dictionary, it then displays the Spelling dialog box and awaits your instructions. You cannot edit the built-in dictionary, but you can add words to Custom.dic so that Excel will not stumble over them in future worksheets. Simply click the Add button in the Spelling dialog box to add the word in the Change To edit box to this dictionary. If you want to use special-purpose dictionaries, create a text-only file (you can use Notepad) with each word you want to include on a separate line, and save the file in the C:\Windows\MSApps\Proof folder with the extension *dic*. Then when you start a spell check for which you want to use the special dictionary, select that dictionary from the Add Words To list when the Spelling dialog box appears. Excel then checks the worksheet against its built-in dictionary as well as the special-purpose dictionary.

Excel suggests possible replacements for the misspelled word in the Suggestions list box and highlights the most likely candidate in the Change To edit box.

3. The suggestion, *Midnight*, is correct, so click the Change All button. The spell checker replaces both instances of the misspelled word and continues checking the document.

4. Complete the spell check, clicking the Ignore or Ignore All button for all the other words that Excel stumbles over.

5. When the spell checker finishes checking the worksheet, it displays a message box. Click OK to return to the worksheet.

Editing Workbooks

Up to now we have been making changes to the information on the worksheets in one workbook. Excel also allows us to move and copy entire worksheets, both within the same workbook and between different workbooks, as you'll see in the following examples.

Inserting and Deleting Worksheets

Suppose we want to insert a worksheet between Sheet1 and Sheet2. Here are the steps:

1. Click Sheet2's tab to make Sheet2 the active worksheet.

2. Choose Worksheet from the Insert menu. Excel inserts a new worksheet called Sheet4 to the left of the active sheet. ←

Inserting sheets

3. Choose Repeat Insert Worksheet from the Edit menu to insert another worksheet. (Check the Edit menu for a Repeat command whenever you want to repeat your previous task.)

Now suppose we want to delete the blank Sheet3. Excel will delete the sheet permanently—there is no Undo safety net. So before we delete a sheet from a workbook, we should always do a quick visual confirmation to verify that we are sending the correct sheet into oblivion. Let's go:

1. Click Sheet3's tab to display that worksheet (it should be blank).

2. Choose Delete Sheet from the Edit menu. Excel warns you that the sheet will be permanently deleted. ←

Deleting sheets

3. Click OK. Excel removes Sheet3 from the 1997 Sales workbook.

4. Press Ctrl+Home to see these results:

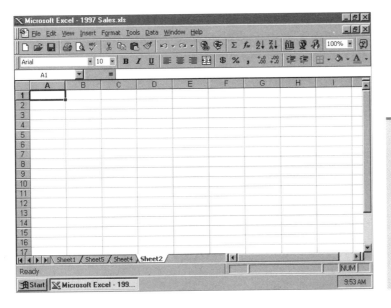

Changing the default number of worksheets

If you often create workbooks with more than three sheets, you can change this default number by choosing Options from the Tools menu and, on the General tab, increasing the Sheets In New Workbook setting.

Naming Sheets

As you can see, when we insert and delete worksheets, Excel does not renumber the sheet tabs, so the tabs are no longer in logical sequence. We can change the names of the sheets to put them back in the correct numerical order, but if we're going to go to all that effort, it makes sense to change the names to something more meaningful than Sheet1, Sheet2, and so on. Here's how to rename the sheets:

1. Double-click the Sheet1 tab to select the text on the tab.

2. Type *Quarterly* and press Enter. Excel displays the new name on the sheet tab.

3. Repeat steps 1 and 2 to rename Sheet 5 as *Totals*, Sheet4 as *Gross Income*, and Sheet2 as *Trial Balance*.

Moving Worksheets

We have already seen how we can effectively "move" a worksheet by moving all its information, but we can also literally move worksheets from one position in a workbook to another. Try this:

1. With the Trial Balance worksheet active, point to its tab and hold down the left mouse button. The pointer changes to an arrow with a sheet attached to it.

2. Drag the sheet pointer until it sits between Totals and Gross Income. Excel indicates with an arrowhead where it will place the Trial Balance sheet.

3. Release the mouse button to move the Trial Balance sheet to its new location.

We can also easily move a worksheet from one workbook to another. To demonstrate, we must first open a new workbook:

The New button

1. Click the New button or choose New from the File menu. Excel displays a new workbook, called Book2.

2. To see both workbooks at the same time, choose Arrange from the Window menu and click OK to accept the default Tiled option. Your screen now looks like this:

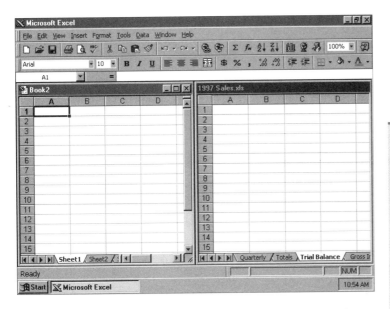

Now we'll move the Trial Balance and Gross Income sheets to Book2:

1. Activate the 1997 Sales workbook, click Trial Balance, and then drag the sheet pointer until it sits to the left of Sheet1 in the Book2 workbook.

2. Repeat step 1 to move the Gross Income sheet between Trial Balance and Sheet1 of Book2.

Copying Worksheets

The procedure for copying information between worksheets in different workbooks is the same as for copying between worksheets in one workbook (see page 30). We can also copy entire sheets both within a workbook and between workbooks. Let's copy the Quarterly sheet to Book2:

1. Activate the Quarterly sheet in 1997 Sales.

2. Point to the Quarterly tab and hold down both the left mouse button and the Ctrl key. The sheet pointer now has a plus sign.

3. Drag the sheet pointer until it sits to the left of Gross Income in Book2 and release both the mouse button and the Ctrl key. Your screen now looks like the one on the next page.

Excel's templates

Excel provides several templates that you can use to create documents such as invoices and purchase orders. To open a template, choose New from the File menu, click the Spreadsheet Solutions tab of the New dialog box, and double-click a template icon. (Some templates are installed by default when you perform a Typical installation. To install additional templates, rerun Excel's Setup program.) After the template opens, you can use the buttons on the template's toolbar to help you fill in the document. You can even click the Display Example/Remove Example button to see an example of a completed document. In addition, you can point to one of the red dots (CellTips) on the template to get help with a particular item. If you want to customize a template—add a company logo or address, for example—click the Customize button in the top right corner of the template, and when the Customize sheet opens, enter the information you want to include in your custom template. To save a custom template, click the Lock/Save Sheet button, select the Lock And Save Template option, and enter a name for your template in the Save Template dialog box.

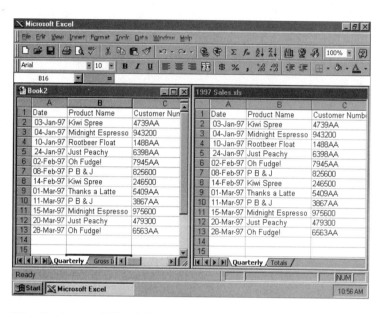

Attaching comments to cells

You might want to attach a comment to a cell for a variety of reasons (to explain a formula or remind yourself to check an assumption, for example). Simply select the cell, choose Comment from the Insert menu, and then type the comment in the text box that appears. (The comment is "signed" with the name entered when Excel was installed on your computer. You can edit or delete this signature.) Click anywhere outside the cell and text box to enter the comment. Excel then places a red marker in the top right corner of each cell with a comment attached. To see a comment, just point to the red marker. To edit or delete a comment, right-click the cell and choose either Edit Comment or Delete Comment from the object menu. (You can also remove comments attached to a selected cell by choosing Clear and then Comments from the Edit menu.)

We don't need Book2 anymore, so let's close it without saving it:

1. Because Book2 is the active workbook, it has a set of buttons at the right end of its title bar. Click the Close button.

2. When Excel asks whether you want to save the changes to Book2, click No.

3. Maximize the 1997 Sales window and save the workbook.

Formatting Basics

Excel offers a variety of formatting options we can use to emphasize parts of a worksheet and display data in different ways. Here we'll look at the common formatting options available on the Formatting toolbar, and we'll take a look at some of the options available in the Format Cells dialog box. We'll also show you a quick way to adjust column widths.

Changing Character Styles

Just as we can use headings to make tables of data easier to read, we can use styles to distinguish different categories of information. Styles change the appearance of the worksheet's characters. For example, we might apply the Bold style to major headings and the Bold and Italic styles to minor headings to make them stand out. Because these character styles are used so often, Excel provides buttons for them. Try this:

1. Select A1:E1, the range that contains the headings.

2. Click the Bold button. The headings are now displayed in bold.

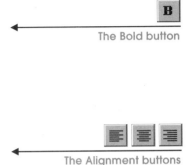

The Bold button

Changing Alignment

As you know, by default Excel left-aligns text and right-aligns values. We can override the default alignment by using the Alignment buttons. Here's how:

1. With A1:E1 still selected, click each Alignment button, noting its effect.

The Alignment buttons

2. When you're ready, click the Center button, which is a typical choice for headings.

Changing Column Widths

In Chapter 1, we widened the columns of the 1997 Sales worksheet by selecting columns, choosing Column Width from the object menu, and setting a width in the resulting dialog box. Adjusting column widths this way can involve some trial and error. In this section, we'll look at other methods that dispense with the guesswork. First let's restore the original column widths:

1. Click the header for column A to select the column. Then point to the header for column E, hold down the Shift key, and click the header. Excel selects columns A through E.

2. Choose Column and then Width from the Format menu to display the dialog box shown earlier on page 18.

3. Type *8.43* in the Column Width edit box and press Enter to return to the worksheet with the selected columns set to the standard width.

   Now let's fine-tune the width of the columns:

1. Press Ctrl+Home to move to cell A1.

Changing the standard width

You can change Excel's standard column width of 8.43 characters by choosing Column and then Standard Width from the Format menu, typing a new value in the Standard Width dialog box, and clicking OK. (Columns whose widths you have already adjusted retain their custom widths.)

Manual adjustment

2. Point to the line between the headers of columns B and C, hold down the left mouse button, drag to the right until column B is wide enough to display all of its entries, and then release the mouse button. (As you drag, Excel displays the width of the column in a pop-up box above the mouse pointer.)

3. Change the width of column C using the same method. Point to the line between the headers of columns C and D. Then hold down the mouse button and drag to the right until column C is wide enough to display its entries.

Now we'll widen column E using a different method:

1. Click column E's header to select the entire column.

Automatic adjustment

2. Choose Column and then AutoFit Selection from the Format menu. Here are the results:

Excel has adjusted the width of the column to its longest entry.

3. Click the Save button to save your changes.

Changing row heights

We can adjust the height of rows the same way we adjust the width of columns. Simply drag the row header's bottom border up or down. We can also choose Row and then Height from the Format menu to make a selected row shorter or taller, or we can choose Row and AutoFit to adjust the height to the tallest entry in a selected row.

Column width shortcut

To quickly adjust the width of a column to fit its longest entry, simply point to the right border of the column's header and double-click.

Wrapping Text in Cells

By default, Excel does not "wrap" text in a cell. As you saw earlier, when we type a long text entry in a cell, that text simply spills over into the adjacent cells instead of wrapping (breaking) to another line within the same cell. Fortunately, Excel provides a way to fit more than one line of text in the same cell, which can be especially useful for aesthetic reasons. For instance, the Customer Number heading in the Quarterly worksheet is much longer than the other entries in column C. We could wrap the heading to two lines and then adjust the width of the column for a more pleasing look. Try the following:

1. Click the row 1 header—the box containing the number 1—to select row 1.

2. Choose Cells from the Format menu and when the Format Cells dialog box appears, click the Alignment tab to display these options:

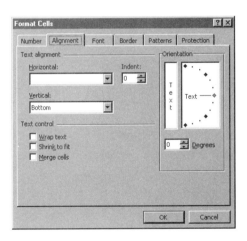

3. Click the Wrap Text box to select that option (the box should contain a check mark), make sure Bottom is selected in the Vertical section, and then click OK. (Turning on the Bottom option ensures that any text in the row that doesn't wrap will sit at the bottom of its cell.)

4. Now point to the dividing line between the headers of columns C and D and drag to the left until the column is slightly wider than the word *Customer*. When you release the mouse button, the worksheet looks like this:

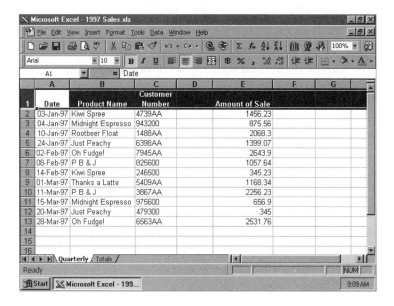

If Number has disappeared, don't panic. Simply choose Row and then AutoFit from the Format menu to ensure that the height of row 1 automatically adjusts to fit the lines of wrapping text.

While we're at it, let's wrap the headings in B1 and E1 too:

1. Use any of the techniques you learned in the previous section to decrease the width of column E so that its heading wraps to two lines.

Forcing text to wrap

2. You can't use this method to wrap the heading in column B because the width of that column is determined by the entries in B2:B13. Instead, force the heading to wrap by double-clicking cell B1, clicking an insertion point just after the word *Product*, pressing Delete to remove the space, and then pressing Alt+Enter to wrap the heading.

3. Press Enter. The results are shown at the top of the facing page.

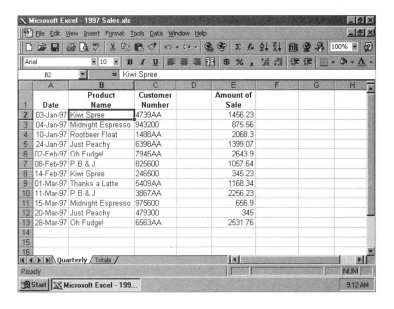

Adding Titles

We've learned how to format headings in simple ways by using buttons on the toolbar to make text bold and change alignment. In this section, we'll get more elaborate. First we'll give the worksheet a title and subtitle that really stand out:

1. Select rows 1, 2, and 3 by dragging down through their headers. Then choose Rows from the Insert menu. Excel inserts the number of rows you have selected—in this case, three—above the selection.

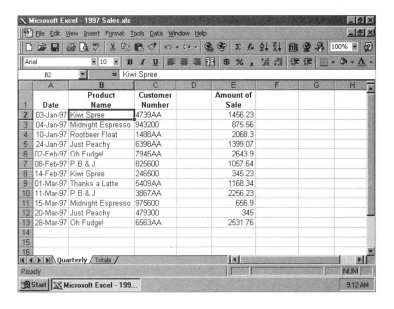

Inserting multiple rows

2. Press Home to remove the highlighting and move to cell A1, type *Preliminary Sales Analysis,* and press the Enter key.

3. In cell A2, type *1st Quarter, 1997* and press Enter.

4. Press Ctrl+Home to select cell A1, and then choose Cells from the Format menu.

5. In the Format Cells dialog box, click the Font tab to display the options shown on the next page.

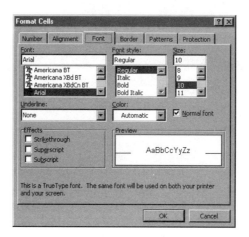

6. Click Bold in the Font Style section, select 22 from the Size list, and click OK. Notice that the height of row 1 increases to accommodate the larger font.

7. Right-click cell A2 and then choose Format Cells from the object menu.

8. In the Format Cells dialog box, click Bold Italic in the Font Style section, select 14 from the Size list, and click OK.

The Merge And Center
button

9. Now let's center the titles across columns A through E. Select A1:E1 and click the Merge And Center button on the Formatting toolbar. Excel centers the title over the selected area and merges the four cells, but the title is still stored in cell A1.

10. Repeat step 9 for the subtitle using the range A2:E2.

Specifying How Values Should Be Displayed

With the exception of the date values in column A, Excel has displayed the values we've entered so far in its default General format. With this format, Excel simply displays what we typed (or what it thinks we typed). For example, when we entered the dates in column A, Excel displayed them in a date format.

Excel provides several formats that we can use to change the way the values look. Try this:

1. Select E5 and click the Comma Style button on the Formatting toolbar. Excel formats the selected cell with a comma and two decimal places.

The Comma Style button

2. Click the Decrease Decimal button a couple of times to round the value in E5 to a whole dollar amount, and then click the Increase Decimal button twice to restore the two decimal places.

The Decrease Decimal and Increase Decimal buttons

3. Finally, click the Currency Style button. Excel adds a dollar sign in front of the value. (If necessary, increase column E's width to view the results.)

The Currency Style button

4. To see the currency format for negative values, enter *1234* in cell F5, enter *–1234* in cell F6, select both values, click the Currency Style button, and click cell F7 to see these results:

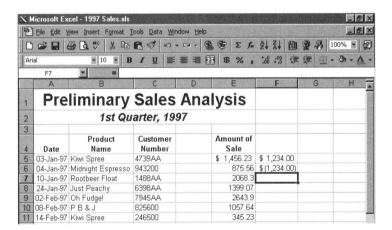

As well as adding a dollar sign, a comma, and two zeros to the right of the decimal point, Excel displays the negative value in parentheses and aligns it with the positive value above it.

When we click the Currency Style button, Excel applies its accounting format, in which the dollar sign is left-aligned, to the selected cells. However, other currency formats are available in the Format Cells dialog box, which also provides several other format options not available as buttons on the Formatting toolbar. Turn the page to see how to apply these other formats.

Underlying vs. displayed

After you apply a format, the value displayed in the cell might look different from the value in the formula bar. For example, 345.6789 is displayed in its cell as $345.68 after you apply the currency format. When performing calculations, Excel uses the value in the formula bar, not the displayed value.

1. Select E6, right-click the selection, and choose Format Cells from the object menu.

2. In the Format Cells dialog box, click the Number tab to display the options shown earlier on page 16.

3. Click each category to view its corresponding options. For example, click Number and note that you can change the number of decimal places, include a comma (1000 separator), and specify the way negative numbers are displayed.

Formatting with styles

Excel applies a combination of formatting called the Normal style to your entries. It replaces Normal with a Currency, Comma, or Percent style when you click those buttons on the Formatting toolbar. You can modify Excel's styles by choosing Style from the Format menu, selecting the style from the Style Name list, and clicking the Modify button to display the Format Cells dialog box, where you can make your changes. To create a custom style, enter a new name in the Style Name edit box, select or deselect the options in the Style Includes list, and use the Modify button to adjust any of the options. Click OK in the Style dialog box to apply the new style to the current selection, or click Add to add the style to the Style Name list without applying it and then click OK. To apply the style later, select a cell or range, choose Style from the Format menu, select the style from the Style Name drop-down list, and then click OK. To delete a style, choose it from the Style Name drop-down list and click the Delete button.

4. Select Currency in the Category list and select the third option in the Negative Numbers list. Be sure the Decimal Places setting is 2 and that $ is selected in the Symbol edit box, and then click OK. Excel formats the selected entry with a dollar sign, a comma, and two decimal places, but as you can see here, the dollar sign is adjacent to the value instead of left-aligned as it is in cell E5:

While we're working with the Number tab of the Format Cells dialog box, you might want to explore Excel's date formats. In Chapter 1, we entered the dates in column A in a variety of formats and later we showed you how to make them all look the same. Let's see what other formats are available:

1. Select A5:A16, right-click the selection, and choose Format Cells from the object menu. Excel displays the Number tab options with the cells' current format highlighted.

2. Select the 4-Mar format and click OK.

3. Return to the Format Cells dialog box and experiment with the other date types.

4. When you're ready, assign the 3/4/97 date type to A5:A16 and click OK.

Copying Styles and Formats

In Excel, we can save a lot of formatting time by copying combinations of styles and formats from one cell to other cells. For example, if we format headings to be bold and centered, we can apply those styles to any cells in the worksheet simply by copying them. Let's give it a try:

1. Select cell F4, type *Type*, and press Enter.

2. Select cell A4, which contains a bold, centered heading, and click the Format Painter button on the Standard toolbar.

The Format Painter button

3. Move the pointer to cell F4 and click once. Excel immediately applies both the bold and centered styles to the selected cell.

Now let's format the remaining values in the Amount of Sale column as currency, this time copying the format from cell E5:

1. Select cell E5 and click the Format Painter button.

2. Next select E6:E16. When you release the mouse button, Excel applies the format from cell E5 to the selected range, adding dollar signs, commas, and two decimal places to the values. Your worksheet looks like this:

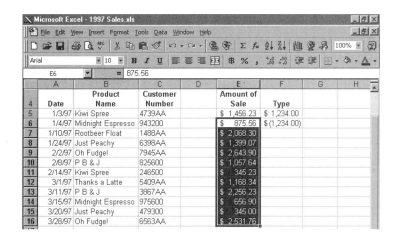

3. Delete the extraneous information in cells F4:F6 and then save your work.

From this simple example, you can see how easy it is to build complex combinations of formatting that can be applied with a couple of clicks of the mouse button.

Printing Worksheets

If our primary purpose in learning Excel is to be able to manipulate our own information, our worksheets might never need to leave our computer. If, on the other hand, we want to share our worksheets with others, we will probably need printed copies. Now is a good time to discuss how to print an Excel worksheet.

Previewing Worksheets

Usually, we'll want to preview a worksheet before we print it to make sure that single-page sheets fit neatly on the page and that multisheet workbooks break in logical places. Follow these steps to get a bird's-eye view of the current worksheet:

The Print Preview button

Page break preview

When you click the Page Break Preview button on the Print Preview toolbar, Excel switches to page break view. You can then adjust where your worksheet's information breaks into pages. Cells that will be printed on the active page appear in white, while cells outside the active page appear in gray. To adjust a page break, simply drag the dotted line that represents the page break to its new location. To return to print preview, click the Print Preview button. To return to normal view, choose Normal from the View menu.

1. With the Quarterly sheet of 1997 Sales displayed on your screen, click the Print Preview button on the Standard toolbar. The print preview window opens, with a miniature version of the printed worksheet displayed, as shown here:

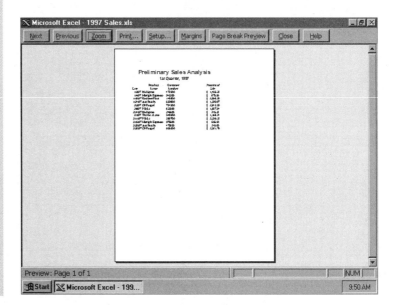

2. Move the mouse pointer over the page. The pointer changes to a small magnifying glass.

3. To examine part of the page in more detail, move the magnifying glass over that part and click the mouse button. Excel zooms in on that portion of the page. Click again to zoom out.

Zooming in and out

Setting Up the Pages

We can change the worksheet's orientation, adjust margins, add a header or footer, and make other adjustments in the Page Setup dialog box. In print preview, we can open this dialog box like this:

1. Click the Setup button on the Print Preview toolbar to display a Page Setup dialog box something like this one:

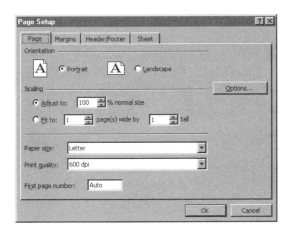

Your dialog box might differ slightly, depending on the type of printer you have. Notice that on the Page tab, you can set the orientation of your printed worksheet and control the scale at which it is printed.

2. Click the Margins tab to display the options shown on the next page.

Adjusting margins in print preview

In addition to using the Margins tab of the Page Setup dialog box, you can also adjust margins and column widths in print preview. Click the Margins button on the Print Preview toolbar to display guidelines that you can manually move to increase or decrease the margins and columns. Click the Margins button again to turn off the guidelines.

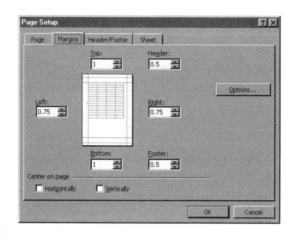

Custom headers and footers

To create a customized header or footer, you can click the Custom Header or Custom Footer button to display a dialog box in which you can type the text you want. The buttons in the Header and Footer dialog boxes add codes that do the following:

&[Page]   Adds current page
           number
&[Pages]   Inserts total number
           of pages
&[Date]   Adds current date
&[Time]   Adds current time
&[File]   Adds filename
&[Tab]   Adds sheet name

Here are some formatting codes:

&b   Prints following
           characters in bold
&i   Italicizes following
           characters
&u   Underlines following
           characters

You can also format headers and footers by selecting the text you want to format, clicking the font button (the capital A) to display the Font dialog box, and making your selections.

In the Center On Page section, click Horizontally and Vertically to center the worksheet horizontally and vertically on the page. The Preview box shows you the effects of your changes.

3. Click OK to return to the print preview window.

Now let's add a header to the worksheet:

1. Click Setup and then click the Header/Footer tab to display these Header/Footer options:

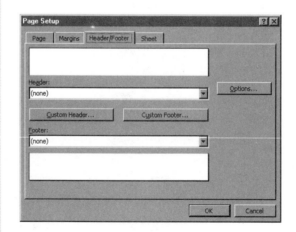

2. Click the arrow to the right of the Header box and select 1997 Sales from the drop-down list.

3. Click the arrow to the right of the Footer box, select Page 1, and click OK. Excel centers the specified text at the top and bottom of the page.

You can also use the Custom Header and Custom Footer buttons to create customized headers and footers; see the tip on the facing page.

Here's how to mark the cell boundaries with gridlines:

1. Click the Setup button and click the Sheet tab to display these options:

Displaying gridlines

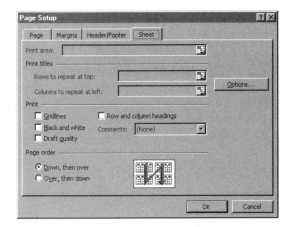

2. Select the Gridlines option in the Print section and then click OK. The worksheet now looks like the one shown on the next page.

Controlling printing

On the Sheet tab of the Page Setup dialog box, you can enter a specific range as the print area of the worksheet. For example, you might want to print only the range containing the results of your calculations. You could select this range before printing and then tell Excel in the Print dialog box to print only the selection, but if you often print the same range, specifying it as the print area is more efficient. (You can also select a range of cells and choose Print Area and then Set Print Area from the File menu. Clear the print area by choosing Print Area and then Clear Print Area.) You can use the options in the Print Titles section of the Sheet tab to tell Excel to repeat column and row headings on multipage worksheets. And you can use options in the Page Order section to tell Excel what order to use when printing multipage worksheets.

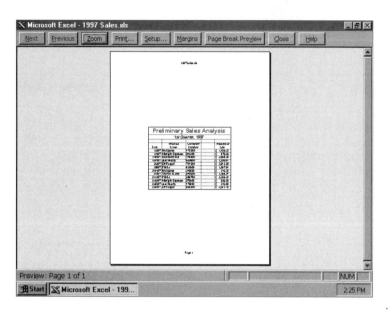

3. Click the Close button on the Print Preview toolbar to return to normal view.

Preparing to Print

The Print button

When we are ready to print, we can click the Print button on the Standard toolbar, or if we want to change the default print settings, we can choose Print from the File menu. Let's try the second method:

1. Choose Print from the File menu to display these options:

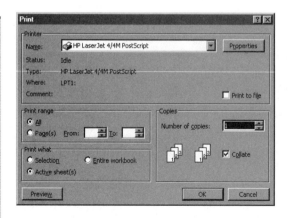

In this dialog box, we can specify exactly what we want to print, from a single cell to an entire workbook. We can also specify the number of copies we want to print, and, if we haven't already paid a visit to print preview, we can activate it directly by clicking the Preview button.

2. To send the worksheet to the printer, click OK. You can then evaluate the results of your efforts on paper.

3 Performing Calculations

This chapter shows you how to build formulas to perform calculations with your data. We create a calculation area and then introduce you to Excel's functions, including the decision-making IF function, and we finish up by consolidating data.

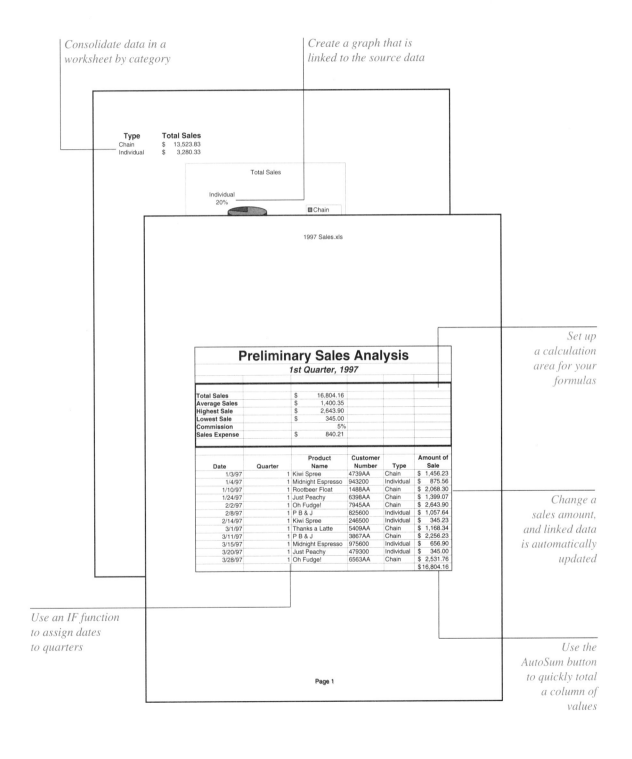

Consolidate data in a worksheet by category

Create a graph that is linked to the source data

Type	Total Sales
Chain	$ 13,523.83
Individual	$ 3,280.33

Total Sales

Individual
20%

■ Chain

1997 Sales.xls

Set up a calculation area for your formulas

Preliminary Sales Analysis
1st Quarter, 1997

		$	
Total Sales		$ 16,804.16	
Average Sales		$ 1,400.35	
Highest Sale		$ 2,643.90	
Lowest Sale		$ 345.00	
Commission		5%	
Sales Expense		$ 840.21	

Date	Quarter	Product Name	Customer Number	Type	Amount of Sale
1/3/97	1	Kiwi Spree	4739AA	Chain	$ 1,456.23
1/4/97	1	Midnight Espresso	943200	Individual	$ 875.56
1/10/97	1	Rootbeer Float	1488AA	Chain	$ 2,068.30
1/24/97	1	Just Peachy	6398AA	Chain	$ 1,399.07
2/2/97	1	Oh Fudge!	7945AA	Chain	$ 2,643.90
2/8/97	1	P B & J	825600	Individual	$ 1,057.64
2/14/97	1	Kiwi Spree	246500	Individual	$ 345.23
3/1/97	1	Thanks a Latte	5409AA	Chain	$ 1,168.34
3/11/97	1	P B & J	3867AA	Chain	$ 2,256.23
3/15/97	1	Midnight Espresso	975600	Individual	$ 656.90
3/20/97	1	Just Peachy	479300	Individual	$ 345.00
3/28/97	1	Oh Fudge!	6563AA	Chain	$ 2,531.76
					$16,804.16

Change a sales amount, and linked data is automatically updated

Use an IF function to assign dates to quarters

Use the AutoSum button to quickly total a column of values

Chapters 1 and 2 covered some Excel basics, and you now know enough to create simple tables. But you are missing the essential piece of information that turns a table into a worksheet: how to enter formulas. The whole purpose of building worksheets is to have Excel perform calculations for us. In this chapter, we show you how to enter formulas in the 1997 Sales workbook to analyze sales. (If you don't work in sales, you can adapt the worksheet to analyze other sources of income such as service fees or subscriptions.) Along the way, we cover some powerful techniques for manipulating data and a few principles of worksheet design. So fire up Excel and then we'll get started.

Simple Calculations

Excel has many powerful functions that are a sort of shorthand for the various formulas used in mathematical, logical, statistical, financial, trigonometric, logarithmic, and other types of calculations. However, the majority of worksheets created with Excel involve simple arithmetic. In this section, we show you how to use four arithmetic operators (+, −, *, and /) to add, subtract, multiply, and divide, and then we introduce two Excel features with which we can quickly add sets of numeric values.

Doing Arithmetic

The = sign

In Excel, we begin a formula with an equal sign (=). In the simplest formulas, the equal sign is followed by a set of values separated by +, −, *, or /, such as

=5+3+2

If we enter this formula in any blank cell in a worksheet, Excel displays the result 10.

Let's experiment with a few formulas. We'll start by inserting a couple of blank rows:

1. In the Quarterly sheet of the 1997 Sales workbook, drag through the headers for rows 4 and 5 to select the two rows.

2. Right-click anywhere in the selected rows and choose Insert from the object menu. Because you selected two rows, Excel inserts two blank rows, moving the table down so that it begins in row 6.

Now we're ready to construct a formula in cell B5, using some of the values in the Amount of Sale column. We tell Excel to use a value simply by clicking the cell that contains it. Follow these steps:

1. Click cell B5 and type an equal sign followed by an opening parenthesis.

2. Click cell E7. Excel inserts the cell reference E7 in the cell and the formula bar. ◄—————— Entering cell references in formulas

3. Type a plus sign and click cell E8. Excel adds the cell reference E8 to the formula.

4. Continue to build the formula by typing plus signs and clicking cells E9, E10, and E11.

5. Type a closing parenthesis followed by a / (the division operator), and then type 5. The formula now looks like this:

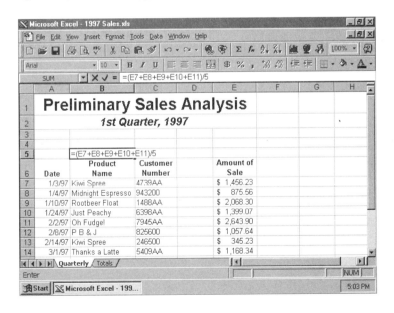

This formula tells Excel to first add the amounts in cells E7, E8, E9, E10, and E11 and then divide the result by 5, to obtain the average of the five amounts.

6. Click the Enter button. Excel displays the result of the formula, 1688.612, in cell B5.

We can use this technique to create any simple formula. Start by typing an equal sign, then enter a value or click the cell that contains the value, type the appropriate arithmetic operator, enter the next value, and so on. Unless we tell Excel to

Order of precedence →

do otherwise, the program performs multiplication and division before addition and subtraction. If we need parts of the formula to be carried out in a different order, use parentheses as we did in this example to override the default order.

Totaling Columns of Values

Although this method of creating a formula is simple enough, it would be tedious to have to type and click to add a long series of values. Fortunately, Excel automates the addition process with a very useful button: the AutoSum button.

Using the AutoSum Button

The AutoSum button →

The AutoSum button will probably become one of your most often-used Excel buttons. In fact, using this button is so easy that we'll dispense with explanations and simply show you what to do:

1. Select cell E19.

Displaying formulas

By default, Excel displays the results of formulas in cells, not their underlying formulas. To see the actual underlying formulas in the worksheet, choose Options from the Tools menu, display the View options, select Formulas in the Window Options section, and click OK. Excel widens the cells so that you can see the formulas. Simply deselect the Formulas option to redisplay the results.

2. Click the AutoSum button on the Standard toolbar. Excel looks first above and then to the left of the active cell for an adjacent range of values to total. Excel assumes that you want to total the values above E19 and enters the SUM function in cell E19 and in the formula bar. Your worksheet looks like the one shown at the top of the facing page.

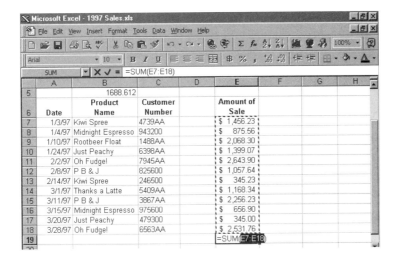

3. Click the Enter button to enter the formula in cell E19. Excel displays the result $16,804.16—the sum of the values in E7:E18.

That was easy. The AutoSum button serves us well whenever we want a total to appear at the bottom of a column or to the right of a row of values. But what if we want the total to appear elsewhere on the worksheet? Knowing how to create SUM functions from scratch gives us more flexibility.

Using the SUM Function

Let's go back and dissect the SUM function that Excel inserted in cell E19 when we clicked the AutoSum button so that we can examine the function's components.

With cell E19 selected, we can see the following entry in the formula bar:

=SUM(E7:E18)

Like all formulas, the SUM function begins with an equal sign (=). Next comes the function name in capital letters, followed by a set of parentheses enclosing the reference to the range containing the amounts we want to total. This reference is the SUM function's *argument*. An argument answers questions such as "What?" or "How?" and gives Excel the additional information it needs to perform the function. In the case of SUM, Excel needs only one piece of information—the references of the cells we want to total. As you'll see later, Excel

Arguments

might need several pieces of information to carry out other functions, and we enter an argument for each piece.

Creating a SUM function from scratch is not particularly difficult. For practice, follow these steps:

1. Select cell B5, and type this:

   =SUM(

   When you begin typing, the cell's old value is overwritten.

2. Select E7:E18 on the worksheet in the usual way. Excel inserts the reference E7:E18 after the opening parenthesis.

3. Type a closing parenthesis and press Enter. Excel displays in cell B5 the total of the values in the Amount of Sale column—$16,804.16.

Referencing Formula Cells in Other Formulas

After we create a formula in one cell, we can use its result in other formulas simply by referencing its cell. To see how this works, follow these steps:

1. Select cell C5 and type an equal sign.

2. Click cell B5, which contains the SUM function you just entered, type a / (the division operator), and then type *12*.

3. Click the Enter button. Excel displays the result—the average of the invoice amounts—in cell C5. (We discuss an easier way to calculate averages on page 70.)

4. Press the Delete key to erase both the experimental formula and its result from cell C5.

Naming Cells and Ranges

Many of the calculations that we might want to perform on this worksheet—for example, calculating each sales amount as a percentage of total sales—will use the total we have calculated in cell B5. We could include a copy of the SUM function now in cell B5 in these other calculations, or we

Function names

When you type a function name, such as SUM, in the formula bar, you don't have to type it in capital letters. Excel capitalizes the function name for you when you complete the entry. If Excel does not respond in this way, you have probably entered the function name incorrectly.

could simply reference cell B5. The latter method seems quick and simple, but what if we subsequently move the formula in B5 to another location? Excel gives us a way to reference this formula no matter where on the worksheet we move it. We can assign cell B5 a name and then use the name in any calculations that involve the total.

We assign a name to a cell by using the Name command on the Insert menu. Follow these steps:

1. Select cell B5 and choose Name and then Define from the Insert menu. Excel displays the Define Name dialog box:

Assigning cell names

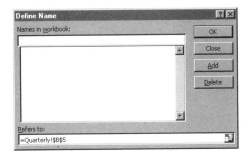

The reference Quarterly!$B$5 is displayed in the Refers To edit box. This absolute reference points to cell B5 on the Quarterly sheet of the current workbook. (For an explanation of absolute references, see page 78.)

2. Type *Total* in the Names In Workbook edit box.

3. Click OK to assign the name Total to cell B5. If you look at the name box to the left of the formula bar, you'll see that Excel now refers to the cell by the name you just entered, instead of by the cell reference B5. You can use either designation in formulas.

To see how Excel uses the names we assign, try this:

1. Select cell E19, which currently contains the SUM function you inserted earlier in the chapter.

2. Type =*Total* and press Enter. The worksheet does not appear to change, but now instead of two SUM functions, the worksheet contains only one. You have told Excel to assign the

Excel's name suggestions

When you choose Name and then Define from the Insert menu to name a cell or a range of cells, Excel looks above and to the left of the selected cell or range to find a name. Keep this information in mind when you enter labels in your worksheet. If you plan on defining names for certain cells, enter a label above or to the left of the cell(s) that Excel can readily use as a name.

value of the cell named Total, which contains the SUM function, to cell E19.

We can also assign names to ranges. Let's assign the name Amount to the cells containing amounts in column E using a different method:

Assigning range names →

1. Select E7:E18 and click the name box to highlight E7.

2. Type *Amount* and press Enter.

Now let's replace the range reference in the SUM function in cell B5 with the new range name:

1. Click B5 to select it and display its contents in the formula bar.

2. Drag through the E7:E18 reference in the formula bar to highlight it. (While you're dragging, Excel displays the reference in blue and outlines the actual range with a blue border.)

Inserting named cells in a formula →

3. Choose Name and then Paste from the Insert menu to display this dialog box:

4. Select Amount and click OK. Excel replaces the range reference with the name assigned to the range, and the formula bar now reads *=SUM(Amount)*.

5. Click the Enter button. The total in cell B5 remains the same as before, even though you've changed the formula.

6. Click the Save button to save your work.

From now on, we won't give you specific instructions to save your work, but you should get in the habit of saving often, perhaps after working through each example.

Name conventions

Certain rules apply when you name cells or ranges. Although you can use a number within the name, you must start the name with a letter, an underscore, or a backslash. Spaces are not allowed within the name, so you should use underscore characters to represent spaces. For example, you cannot use 1997 as a name, but you can use Totals_1997.

Creating a Calculation Area

Before we discuss other calculations we might want to perform with this worksheet, let's look at ways to format our information to make the results of calculations stand out from the data. As your worksheets grow in complexity, you'll find that paying attention to such details will keep you oriented and help others understand your results.

Usually when we create a worksheet, we are interested not so much in the individual pieces of information as in the results of the calculations we perform on the pieces. The current worksheet is not much bigger than one screen, but often worksheets of this type include many screenfuls of information. It's a good idea to design our worksheets so that the important information is easily accessible and in a predictable location. For these reasons, we leave room in the top left corner of our worksheets for a calculation area. This habit is useful for the following reasons:

- We don't have to scroll around looking for totals and other results.   ← *Advantages*

- We can print just the first page of a worksheet to get a report of the most pertinent information.

- We can easily jump to the calculation area from anywhere on the worksheet by pressing Ctrl+Home to move to cell A1.

Let's create an area at the top of the Quarterly sheet of the 1997 Sales workbook for a set of calculations. We'll start by freeing up some more space below the worksheet title:

1. Select A6:E19 and use the Cut and Paste buttons to move the selection to A13:E26. (Leave the entry in B5 where it is.)

2. Press Ctrl+Home. Your screen now looks as shown on the next page.

Jumping to named cells

To move quickly to a named cell, press the F5 key. When Excel displays the Go To dialog box, select the name of the cell you want to move to and click OK.

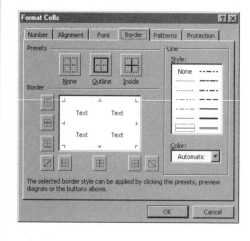

Setting off areas with repeating characters

Another way to set off a block of cells is with a line of repeating characters. A quick way to enter repeating characters is to use Excel's Fill option, which is not to be confused with Excel's Fill command (see the tip on page 76). For example, to fill the range A3:E3 with asterisks, type an asterisk in cell A3, select the range A3:E3, choose Cells from the Format menu, click the Alignment tab of the Format Cells dialog box, select Fill from the Horizontal drop-down list, and click OK. Excel then fills A3:E3 with a line of asterisks. You can also experiment with combinations of characters, such as asterisk-hyphen-asterisk, to create different effects. Using the Fill option as described here is more efficient than typing countless characters, not only because it saves typing time but also because the Fill option responds to changes you make to column widths. For example, if you decrease the width of column A, Excel adjusts the number of asterisks so that they continue to fill the selected range.

Now we'll set off the calculation area. With Excel, we can get really fancy, using colored fonts and shading to draw attention to calculation results. For now, though, let's place a simple border around the calculation area:

1. Select A4:E11 and choose Cells from the Format menu.

2. When the Format Cells dialog box appears, click the Border tab to display these options:

3. In the Style section, select the second to last option in the column on the right, and in the Presets section, select Outline.

4. Click OK to apply the border to the selected range.

Now let's add another touch:

1. Select A5:A10 and click the Bold button on the Formatting toolbar.   ← Preformatting cells

Why did we tell you to select the empty cells before applying the Bold style? Try this:

1. Select cell A5, type *Total Sales*, and click the Enter button. The new heading is bold because you already applied the Bold style to cell A5.

2. Without moving the selection, choose Column and AutoFit Selection from the Format menu to adjust the width of column A to the longest entry. (From now on, use this technique to adjust columns as necessary to see their contents.)

3. For good measure, select cell E14, click the Format Painter button, and select B5:B10 to copy the currency format to that range of cells.

4. Press Ctrl+Home. Here's the result of your formatting:

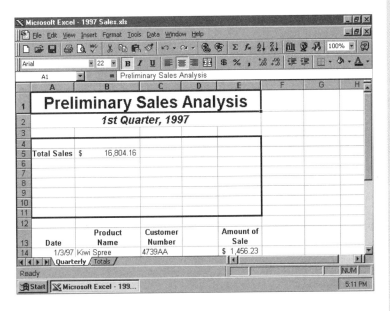

Page breaks

If you want to print the calculation area on one page and the supporting data on another, or if you need to control where the pages break in a multipage worksheet, select the cell below the row and to the right of the column at which you want Excel to break the page, and choose Page Break from the Insert menu. Excel indicates the break with a dashed line. To remove a manual page break, select the cell immediately below and to the right of the page break, and choose Remove Page Break from the Insert menu. To remove all the page breaks in a worksheet, select the entire document by clicking the square in the top left corner of the worksheet (at the intersection of the row and column headers), and then choose Remove Page Break.

More Calculations

Let's perform some more calculations on the sales data, starting with the average sales.

Averaging Values

To find the average of the invoices in this worksheet, we'll use Excel's AVERAGE function. We'll use the Paste Function button on the Standard toolbar to avoid making errors while typing function names and to make sure we include all the arguments needed for the calculation. Follow these steps:

1. Select cell A6, type *Average Sales*, and click the Enter button. If the heading has wrapped to two lines, right-click the cell, choose Format Cells, and on the Alignment tab, turn off Wrap Text, and click OK. Then widen the cell.

The Paste Function button

2. Select cell B6 and click the Paste Function button. Excel displays the Paste Function dialog box shown below. (If necessary, close the Office Assistant.)

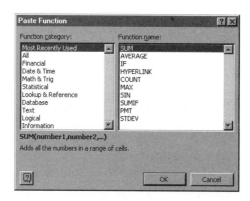

Below the list boxes, the dialog box displays the syntax of the selected function. The syntax tells you how the function must be entered after the = sign in the formula bar. You will replace the placeholders between parentheses in the syntax—in this case, *number1,number2,...*—with the actual values you want Excel to use.

3. Select AVERAGE in the Function Name list and click OK. Excel displays this formula palette:

Conditional formatting

To monitor a worksheet, you can use conditional formatting to highlight a cell that meets certain criteria. For example, you can display a cell's value in magenta if it is over 200,000. To apply this type of formatting, select the cell and choose Conditional Formatting from the Format menu. Select a condition from the second drop-down list and enter conditional parameters in the appropriate edit boxes. Then click Format, select the formatting to be used to highlight the cell, and click OK twice. When the value in the selected cell meets the condition you've set, Excel highlights the cell with the specified formatting. To delete conditional formatting, select the cell, choose Conditional Formatting from the Format menu, click Delete, select the condition, and click OK twice.

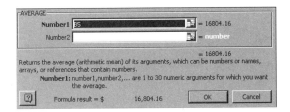

The palette displays a definition of the function and its arguments. In the Number1 edit box, you can enter a number, cell reference, name, formula, or another function.

4. Click the Collapse button (the button with the red arrow at the right end of the Number1 edit box) to shrink the palette. Then select E14:E25 in the worksheet to add its name, Amount, as the formula's argument.

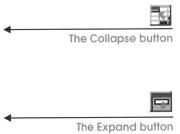

The Collapse button

The Expand button

5. Click the Expand button (the button with the red arrow) to enlarge the palette, as shown here:

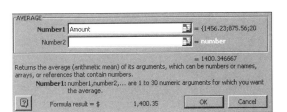

6. Click OK to enter the formula in cell B6 and press Ctrl+Home to see the results. Excel displays $1,400.35 in cell B6.

Identifying Highest and Lowest Values

Excel provides two functions that instantly identify the highest and lowest values in a group. To understand the benefits of these functions, imagine that the Quarterly worksheet contains data from not 12 but 112 customers! Let's start with the highest sale:

1. Select cell A7, type *Highest Sale*, and press the Right Arrow key to confirm the entry and select cell B7.

2. Click the Edit Formula button (the = at the left end of the formula bar). Excel enters = in the formula bar and replaces the name box with the function name box.

Moving dialog boxes

To enter a cell or range reference in a dialog box, you can click the cell or select the range in the worksheet. If the dialog box obscures the desired cell or range, simply move the dialog box out of the way by pointing to its title bar, holding down the mouse button, and dragging until you can see the part of the worksheet you're interested in. Many dialog boxes also contain Collapse buttons (the buttons with the red arrow) that shrink the dialog box down so that you can view more of the worksheet.

3. Click the arrow to the right of the function name box and select MAX (for *maximum*) from the Function Name list. (If MAX is already displayed, simply click MAX.) Excel then displays the formula palette shown here:

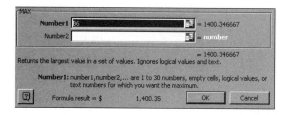

4. Click the Collapse button at the right end of the Number 1 edit box to shrink the palette, and select E14:E25 on the worksheet. The formula bar displays =MAX(Amount).

5. Click the Expand button to redisplay the formula palette and notice that Excel displays the result of the formula at the bottom of the dialog box.

6. Click OK to close the formula palette. Excel enters the highest sale amount, $2,643.90, in cell B7.

To determine the lowest sale, we'll use Excel's AutoCalculate feature:

1. Select cell A8, type *Lowest Sale*, and press Enter.

2. Select E14:E25, right-click the AutoCalculate area in the status bar (refer to the figure on page 5), and select Min from the object menu. Excel displays the result, $345.00, in the AutoCalculate area.

3. Now that you know the result, select cell B8, type *345*, and press Enter.

We can also use AutoCalculate to quickly apply other functions, such as AVERAGE and COUNT, to a selected range.

Calculating with Names

The salespeople at the Cream of the Crop ice cream company all earn commission. As a gross indicator of sales expenses,

A function for every task

Excel provides many functions for common business and financial tasks—some of them quite complex. To get more information about a function, choose Contents And Index from the Help menu. Then type *worksheet functions* on the Index tab and double-click List Of to display the Topics Found dialog box, which lists categories of worksheet functions. Double-click the category you are interested in (such as About Financial Functions), scroll the Help window, and then click a specific function (such as RATE). Excel displays a description of the function, its syntax, and any other pertinent information.

we can use the Total Sales value in cell B5 to calculate the total sales commission. Here's how:

1. In cell A9, type *Commission* and press Tab.

2. Type *6%* and click the Enter button.

3. With cell B9 still active, choose Name and then Define from the Insert menu. Excel scans the adjacent cells and suggests the name *Commission*. Click OK.

Now we'll use the commission percentage in a formula that will calculate the total commission:

1. Select cell A10, type *Sales Expense*, and press Tab.

2. With cell B10 selected, type the formula *=Total*Commission* and press Enter. Excel multiplies the value in the cell named Total (B5) by the value in the cell named Commission (B9) and displays the result, $1,008.25, in cell B10.

3. Now select cell B9, type *5%*, and press Enter. Instantly, the value in cell B10 changes to reflect the new commission rate, as shown here:

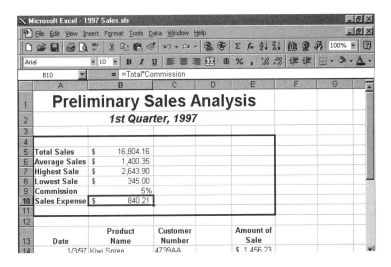

If a hundred calculations throughout the worksheet referenced the cell named Commission, Excel would adjust all their results to reflect this one change. Powerful stuff!

Formulas That Make Decisions

There will be times when we want Excel to carry out one task under certain circumstances and another task if those circumstances don't apply. To give this kind of instruction to Excel, we use the IF function.

Using the IF Function

How the IF function works

In its simplest form, the IF function tests the value of a cell and does one thing if the test is positive (true) and another if the test is negative (false). It requires three arguments: the test, the action to perform if the test is true, and the action to perform if the test is false. We supply the arguments one after the other within the function's parentheses, separating them with commas (no spaces). Try this:

1. Select cell D5, type the following, and then press Enter:

   =IF(B5=0,"TRUE","FALSE")

   Excel checks whether the value in cell B5 is zero (the test), and because it isn't zero, it ignores TRUE (the action to perform if the test is true) and displays FALSE (the action to perform if the test is false) in cell D5.

2. Double-click cell D5. (Notice that Excel changes the B5 reference to blue and puts a matching blue border around cell B5—see the tip on the facing page for more information.) Drag through =0 to highlight it, type *<100000*, and press Enter. The entry in cell D5 instantly changes from FALSE to TRUE, because the value in cell B5 is less than one hundred thousand; that is, the test is true.

3. Now select cell D5 and press Delete to clear the cell.

In this example, the test Excel performed was a simple evaluation of the value in a cell. However, we can also build tests that involve other functions. Recall that the last two characters of the customer numbers in column C of the worksheet indicate whether the sale was made to a large chain store or to an individually-owned store. Suppose we want to assign Chain and Individual entries to each customer number

Logical operators

Here is a list of operators you can use with the IF function:

= < > <> >= <=

You can also use AND and OR to combine two or more tests. The function

=IF(AND(B4=0,B5>0),"Yes","No")

displays Yes only if both tests are true. The function

=IF(OR(B4=0,B5>0),"Yes","No")

displays Yes if either test is true.

so that we can compare the sales for the two store types. Follow these steps:

1. Select cell D13, enter the heading *Type*, and press Enter.

2. In cell D14, type the following and click the Enter button:

   =IF(RIGHT(C14,2)="AA","Chain","Individual")

You have told Excel to look at the two characters at the right end of the value in cell C14 and if they are AA, to enter *Chain* in cell D14. If they are not AA, Excel is to enter *Individual*. The result is shown here:

Using Nested IF Functions

When constructing conditions, we can use IF functions within IF functions. Called *nested functions*, these formulas add another dimension to the complexity of the decisions Excel can make. Here's a quick demonstration:

1. Insert a new column between columns A and B by selecting cell B3 and choosing Columns from the Insert menu. (You can't select the cells above B3 or the entire column B before inserting the new column because B1 and B2 contain merged cells.) Then enter the column heading *Quarter* in cell B13.

Range Finder

When you double-click a cell to edit a formula, Excel's Range Finder feature displays any of the formula's cells or ranges of cells in a particular color and places a matching color border around the actual cell or range. The Range Finder is a useful means of double-checking the references in your formulas.

2. Select B14:B25, right-click the selection, choose Format Cells from the object menu, click the Number tab, select General from the Category list, and click OK.

3. Now select cell B14 and type this formula all on one line:

Functions within functions →

$$=IF(MONTH(A14)<4,1,IF(MONTH(A14)<7,2,$$
$$IF(MONTH(A14)<10,3,4)))$$

4. Check your typing, paying special attention to all the parentheses, and then click the Enter button. (Notice that as you type, Excel color codes sets of parentheses so that you can be sure you have entered the correct number of parentheses.)

You have told Excel to check the month component of the date in cell A14. If it is less than 4, Excel is to display 1 in the corresponding cell in the Quarter column. If the month is not less than 4 but is less than 7, Excel is to display 2 in the Quarter column. If it is not less than 7 but is less than 10, Excel is to display 3. Otherwise, Excel is to display 4. If you have typed the formula correctly, Excel enters 1 in cell B14.

Copying Formulas

The IF functions we just entered are arduous to type, even for good typists. Fortunately, we don't have to enter them more than once. By using AutoFill, we can copy the formula into the cells below, like this:

1. With B14 selected, position the pointer over the fill handle in the bottom right corner of the cell.

2. Hold down the mouse button and drag down to cell B25. Excel copies the formula from B14 into the highlighted cells.

3. Select cell E14 and position the pointer over the fill handle in the bottom right corner of that cell.

4. Hold down the mouse button and drag down to cell E25. The worksheet now looks like the one shown here:

The Fill command

You can use the Fill command to copy entries into a range of adjacent cells. Select the cell whose contents and formats you want to copy, drag through the adjacent range, and choose Fill from the Edit menu. How Excel copies the cell is determined by the shape of the selection and the command you choose from the Fill submenu. For example, selecting cells below an entry and choosing Down copies the entry down a range; selecting cells to the right of an entry and choosing Right copies the entry to the right; and so on. Three related commands are also available on this submenu: Across Worksheets copies entries to the equivalent cells in a group of selected worksheets (to select the worksheets, hold down Ctrl and click each sheet's tab); Series fills the selection with a series of values or dates; and Justify distributes the contents of the active cell evenly in the cells of the selected range.

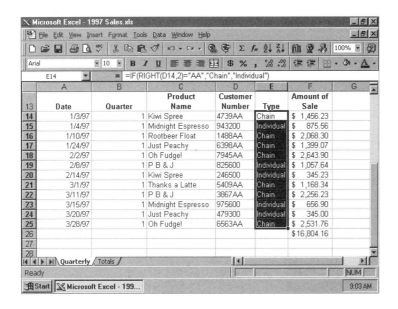

5. With cell E14 selected, look at the formula in the formula bar. Excel has changed the original formula

=IF(RIGHT(C14,2)="AA","Chain","Individual")

to

=IF(RIGHT(D14,2)="AA","Chain","Individual")

Excel changed the reference to account for the addition of the Quarter column. If you click cell E15, you'll see that when you used AutoFill, Excel changed the reference so that it refers to cell D15 as its argument, not D14. Why?

By default, Excel uses *relative references* in its formulas. Relative references refer to cells by their position in relation to the cell containing the formula. So when we copied the formula in cell E14 to cell E15, Excel changed the reference from D14 to D15—the cell in the same row and one column to the left of the cell containing the formula. If we were to copy the formula in cell E14 to F14, Excel would change the reference from D14 to E14 so that the formula would continue to reference the cell in the same relative position.

Text values as arguments

When entering text values as arguments in a formula, you must enclose them in quotation marks. Otherwise, Excel thinks the text is a name and displays the error value #NAME? in the cell. For example,

=RIGHT("Excel",2)

gives the value "el," but

=RIGHT(Excel,2)

results in an error—unless the range name *Excel* happens to be assigned to a cell or range in the worksheet.

Absolute references

When we don't want a reference to be copied as a relative reference, as it was in these examples, we need to use an *absolute reference*. Absolute references refer to cells by their fixed position in the worksheet. To make a reference absolute, we add dollar signs before its column letter and row number. For example, to change the reference C4:C9 to an absolute reference, we would enter it as $C$4:$C$9. We could then copy a formula that contained this reference anywhere on the worksheet and it would always refer to the range C4:C9.

References can also be partially relative and partially absolute. For example, $C3 has an absolute column reference and a relative row reference, and C$3 has a relative column reference and an absolute row reference.

Consolidating Data

So far, the calculations we have performed in this chapter have been pretty straightforward. In this section, we'll take a look at Excel's Consolidate command, which enables us to summarize data in a variety of ways. Suppose we want to total the sales amounts on the Quarterly sheet of the 1997 Sales workbook by store type, but instead of putting the totals on the same sheet, we want to enter them on a separate worksheet and create a link between the totals and their source data so that if the data changes, the totals will, too. This task seems pretty complicated, but it's simple with Excel. Follow the steps below:

1. Click the Totals tab to display that sheet, and enter the heading *Type* in cell A1 and the heading *Total Sales* in cell B1. Make the headings bold, size 12, and centered, and adjust the widths of the columns as necessary.

2. Select cell A2 and choose Consolidate from the Data menu to display this dialog box:

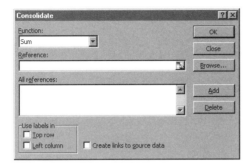

3. In the worksheet window, click the Quarterly tab. Excel enters the name of that sheet in the Reference box.

4. Click the Collapse button at the top right end of the Reference box, select E14:F25, and click the Expand button. Excel has added an absolute reference to the selected range to the Reference box.

5. If Sum does not already appear in the Function edit box, select it from the Function drop-down list.

6. In the Use Labels In section, select the Left Column option to tell Excel to use the entries in the Type column on the Quarterly sheet as labels on the Totals sheet. (Excel redisplays the Totals sheet at this point.)

7. Select Create Links To Source Data to link the data in the Totals sheet to the data in the Quarterly sheet, and click OK to perform the consolidation. The results (after we widened column A and pressed Ctrl+Home) are shown on the next page.

Consolidating data from multiple worksheets

To consolidate data from more than one worksheet, the data in each of the source worksheets must be arranged in the same way. For example, if customer names are in column B in Sheet1, they must be in column B in Sheet2, Sheet3, Sheet4, and so on. Furthermore, all of the worksheets must contain the same customer names in the same order. The next step involves setting up a consolidation worksheet, like the Totals sheet in the chapter example. Once that is complete, all you have to do is select the destination area in the consolidation worksheet, choose Consolidate from the Data menu, select a function (such as Sum), and enter a reference to each of the source worksheets (after you enter a reference, click the Add button to add the reference to the All References list). When you click OK, Excel performs the consolidation, assembling the data from the source worksheets in the consolidation worksheet. (Note that the source worksheets can be in the same workbook or in different workbooks.) For example, if you maintain an income summary by customer for each month, you can consolidate the data in the twelve monthly sheets into an annual income summary by customer.

Excel has entered the column labels in the Type column and the totals in the Total Sales column, which is now column C. Excel inserted a column and outlined the worksheet to hide the mechanisms used to maintain the link between the totals and their source data. (For more about outlining worksheets, see the tip below.) Let's display the hidden information:

1. Click the small button with the plus sign to the left of the row 9 header to display the underlying data for chain store totals. Then click the plus sign button to the left of the row 15 header to display the data for the individual store totals.

2. Now click the small button with the number 1 in the top left corner of the worksheet to again hide all the underlying (second level) data and display only the consolidated (first level) data.

Graphing Consolidated Data

We cover graphs in the following chapter, but we'll quickly introduce them here. Using the consolidated data in the Totals sheet, let's create a pie graph to show what percentages of Cream of the Crop's sales went to chain stores and individually-owned stores. Follow these steps:

Outlining worksheets

Excel's outlining feature lets you view as little or as much of a worksheet as you want to see. To outline a worksheet, select all the cells containing data and choose Group And Outline and then Auto Outline from the Data menu. Excel searches for what it considers to be the most important information (for example, the totals) and uses this information to create different row and column outline levels. Initially, an outlined worksheet displays all its levels. You use the row level buttons and column level buttons in the top left corner of the window to expand and collapse the outline. For example, clicking the 2 row level button displays only the first and second levels and hides any lower levels. You can also click the buttons marked with minus signs above and to the left of the worksheet to collapse an outline level. Excel deduces that the last row or column of a section is the "bottom line" of the collapsed section and displays only that row or column. Conversely, you can click the buttons marked with plus signs to expand collapsed levels. Choose Group And Outline and then Clear Outline to leave outline mode.

1. Select A1:A15 in the Totals sheet. Then hold down the Ctrl key and select C1:C15. (By holding down the Ctrl key, you can select noncontiguous blocks of cells.)

Selecting noncontiguous ranges

The Chart Wizard button

2. Click the Chart Wizard button to display the first of four dialog boxes that lead you through the process of creating and customizing a graph:

3. Select Pie from the Chart Type list and select 3-D Pie in the Chart Sub-Type section (the second option in the top row). Then click Next to display this dialog box:

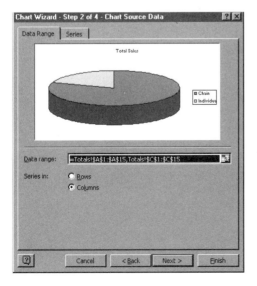

The Chart Wizard displays how the selected range will look as a graph, with all labels and other information in place.

4. Click Next and then click the Data Labels tab to display this dialog box:

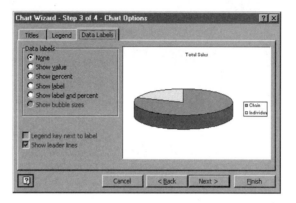

5. Click the Show Label And Percent option and then click Finish to skip the remaining dialog box, thereby accepting the Chart Wizard's default settings for a 3-D pie graph. (We'll walk you through all the Chart Wizard's dialog boxes in the next chapter.) The results are shown here:

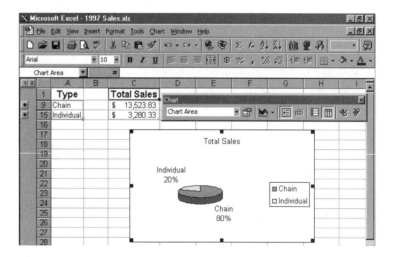

Recall that earlier we created a link between the Quarterly sheet and the Totals sheet when we selected the Create Links To Source Data option in the Consolidate dialog box. To test the validity of that link, follow these steps:

1. Display the Quarterly sheet and change the entry in F15 to $10,000.

2. Now display the Totals sheet and check that the individual store total has changed from $3,280.33 to $12,404.77. Note too that the graph has been updated: The individual store sales now account for 48% of all ice cream sales!

3. Before you continue on to the next chapter, redisplay the Quarterly sheet and restore the entry in cell F15 to $875.56. (You might want to check the Totals sheet again to be sure that it has been updated as well.)

As you can see by this simple example, creating links between worksheets can really save us time. All we have to do is update the source worksheet, and Excel updates any linked worksheets for us. We'll see another example of the power of linked worksheets in Chapter 6.

PART TWO

BUILDING PROFICIENCY

In Part Two, we build on the techniques you learned in Part One to create even more sophisticated workbooks. After completing these chapters, you will be able to create many types of business worksheets. In Chapter 4, you learn how to set up worksheets to take advantage of Excel's autoformats, and then you plot various types of graphs. In Chapter 5, we show you how to work with databases of information, which Excel calls lists. In Chapter 6, we wrap up the book with a set of more advanced calculations that involve linked workbooks, including iteration and three types of what-if analysis: goal-seeking, data tables, and scenarios.

Visually Presenting Data

4

Excel's sophisticated autoformats and graphing capabilities help you analyze a budget by displaying its components visually. We create a graph on the worksheet and then format it in a variety of ways. Finally, we preview and print the graph.

Instantly format a worksheet
with an autoformat

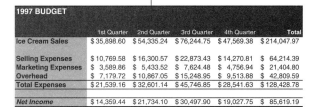

1997 BUDGET					
	1st Quarter	2nd Quarter	3rd Quarter	4th Quarter	Total
Ice Cream Sales	$ 35,898.60	$ 54,335.24	$ 76,244.75	$ 47,569.38	$ 214,047.97
Selling Expenses	$ 10,769.58	$ 16,300.57	$ 22,873.43	$ 14,270.81	$ 64,214.39
Marketing Expenses	$ 3,589.86	$ 5,433.52	$ 7,624.48	$ 4,756.94	$ 21,404.80
Overhead	$ 7,179.72	$ 10,867.05	$ 15,248.95	$ 9,513.88	$ 42,809.59
Total Expenses	$ 21,539.16	$ 32,601.14	$ 45,746.85	$ 28,541.63	$ 128,428.78
Net Income	$ 14,359.44	$ 21,734.10	$ 30,497.90	$ 19,027.75	$ 85,619.19

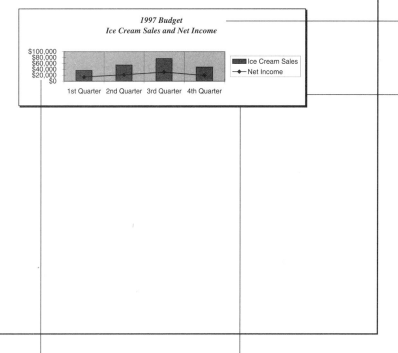

Easily add and
format a title

Plot data
with the help of
Microsoft
Graph

Scale the axes to
maximize legibility

Frame the graph to
anchor it on the page

In Part One, you learned enough about Excel to put the program to use in your own work. After all that effort, let's relax a bit in this chapter. Using a budget worksheet as a basis, we'll explore various ways we can visually present worksheet data.

Setting Up a Budget

Before we can start, we need to set up this projected budget worksheet for the Cream of the Crop ice cream company:

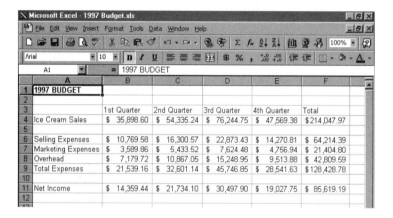

Once the worksheet is in place, we can plot the budget information as various kinds of graphs. Assuming that you have already started Excel, follow these steps to create the worksheet:

1. Close any open workbooks by choosing Close from the File menu or by clicking the workbook's Close button. Then click the New Workbook button on the toolbar.

2. Save the blank workbook as *1997 Budget*. From now on, save the workbook frequently as you build the budget.

3. In cell A1 of Sheet1, type *1997 BUDGET*, click the Enter button to enter the title, and click the Bold button to make the title bold.

4. In cell B3, type *1st Quarter* and click the Enter button. Using AutoFill, drag the fill handle to cell E3 (see page 31 and the adjacent tip for more information about AutoFill). Excel automatically fills the range with the headings *2nd Quarter*, *3rd Quarter*, and *4th Quarter*. Finally, enter *Total* in cell F3.

Filling cells with a series of labels

5. In cell A4, type *Ice Cream Sales* and press Right Arrow.

6. Next, enter these sales amounts in the indicated cells:

B4	*35898.60*
C4	*54335.24*
D4	*76244.75*
E4	*47569.38*

Now let's tackle the expenses. To simplify the data-entry process for this example, let's assume that we have selling expenses that average 30 percent of sales, marketing expenses that average 10 percent of sales, and overhead expenses (fixed costs) that average 20 percent. Follow these steps:

1. Enter the following information in the indicated cells:

A6	*Selling Expenses*
A7	*Marketing Expenses*
A8	*Overhead*
A9	*Total Expenses*
A11	*Net Income*
B6	*=.3*B4*
B7	*=.1*B4*
B8	*=.2*B4*
B9	*=SUM(B6:B8)*

For the entry in cell B9, you can either enter the SUM function from the keyboard or click the AutoSum button.

2. Select B6:B9 and drag the fill handle across to column E to duplicate the 1st quarter formulas for the 2nd, 3rd, and 4th quarters.

3. Select B4:F11 and click the Currency Style button on the Formatting toolbar.

More about AutoFill

You can copy information from one area of your worksheet to another using two methods: AutoFill, and copy and paste. These methods produce similar results unless the entry you are copying contains a number that can be incremented, such as in the 1st Quarter heading, or the cell contains an entry from a custom list. If the cell contains a number that can be incremented, using AutoFill copies the entry and increments the number—for example, 1st Quarter becomes 2nd Quarter, 3rd Quarter, and so on. If the cell contains an entry from a custom list, Excel fills the cells with other entries from that list. You define a custom list by choosing Options from the Tools menu, clicking the Custom Lists tab, selecting NEW LIST in the Custom Lists box, and typing the list's entries in the List Entries box. (You can also click an insertion point in the Import List From Cells edit box, select a range containing the entries, and click the Import button to import the entries as a list.) After you click OK, you can enter the list in consecutive cells of any worksheet by typing one of the entries and dragging the fill handle. This feature is invaluable if you frequently create worksheets involving lists of the same entries, such as part numbers or employee names.

4. Widen column A so that all its labels are visible. Drag through the headers for columns B through E and choose Column and then Width from the Format menu. When the Column Width dialog box appears, type *12* in the Column Width edit box and click OK. All four selected columns take on the new width.

Now, let's compute the Total column and Net Income row:

1. In cell B11, type *=B4–B9* and click the Enter button. Excel enters the result, $14,359.44, as the 1st Quarter's net income.

2. Use AutoFill to copy the formula in cell B11 to C11:F11.

3. Select cell F4, click the AutoSum button, and click the Enter button.

4. Point to the bottom border of cell F4, hold down Ctrl, and drag the cell image to F6. When you release the mouse button and Ctrl key, Excel copies the SUM function to the specified location.

5. Use AutoFill to copy the formula in cell F6 to F7:F9.

Voilà! The worksheet looks like the one shown on page 88.

Automatic Formatting

We have seen that we can use combinations of fonts and styles to draw attention to important worksheet details. Now let's look at a powerful Excel feature designed to make short work of worksheet formatting: *autoformats*. An autoformat is a predefined combination of formatting that works well with worksheets like the one we just created to produce fancy-looking reports with the click of a button. Try this:

Autoformats

1. Select A1:F11 and choose AutoFormat from the Format menu. Excel displays this dialog box:

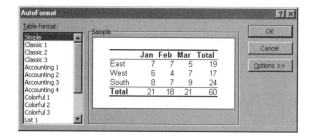

2. In the Table Format list, find and select 3D Effects 1, click OK, and then click anywhere outside the table. Here's the impressive result:

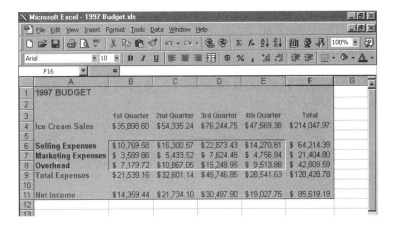

3. Click the Print button to print the budget data.

4. Select A1:F11 again and choose AutoFormat from the Format menu. Select Colorful 2 from the Table Format list and click OK to produce another eye-catching report.

5. Try some of the other autoformats, finishing with Classic 2.

The autoformats that come with Excel don't work well unless the worksheet is set up with them in mind. Nevertheless, they are a great way to become familiar with the many effects we can create with combinations of fonts, lines, colors, and shading. If you don't find a format that produces exactly the look you want, you can assign an autoformat as a starting point and then make refinements using the Font, Fill Color, Font Color, and Borders buttons on the Formatting toolbar or the options available in the Format Cells dialog box.

Plotting Graphs

With Excel, we can create graphs in three ways: on the current worksheet, as a separate sheet in the current workbook, or in another workbook. In this section, we'll quickly plot the budget data on the current worksheet. The advantage of this method is that we can then print the graph and the underlying worksheet on the same page. When we create a graph in

Removing worksheet autoformats

If you decide not to use a worksheet autoformat after all, select the formatted range, choose Auto-Format from the Format menu, select None from the Table Format list, and click OK.

Microsoft Graph →

Excel, a graphing program called Microsoft Graph actually does all the work. (Graph ships with Excel and is installed when we perform a Typical installation.) Here, we'll use Graph in conjunction with the Chart Wizard to create a few graphs. Don't be concerned if your graphs don't look exactly the same as ours. Differences in screen setups or the order of selecting functions can change the way graphs display.

When we create a graph from a selected range of data in a worksheet, Excel maintains a link between the worksheet and the graph. This link is dynamic: If we make changes to the worksheet data, Graph revises the graph to reflect the new data. We can create more than one graph from the same range of data, and the data can be arranged either in columns or rows.

The first graph we'll create is a column-oriented graph. Follow these steps:

1. Select A6:E8 on Sheet1 of the 1997 Budget workbook and click the Chart Wizard button.

2. The Chart Wizard displays the dialog box shown earlier on page 81. This is the first of four dialog boxes that will lead you through the process of creating and customizing a graph.

Creating graphs on chart sheets

To create a graph on a separate chart sheet, build the graph in the Chart Wizard's dialog boxes as usual and then select the As New Sheet option in the fourth Chart Wizard dialog box. In the adjacent edit box, you can type in a name for the new sheet or leave it as the default, *Chart1*. When you click Finish, Excel inserts a chart sheet in front of the active worksheet and plots the graph on the new sheet. To quickly build a graph in the default format on a separate chart sheet, simply select the worksheet data you want to plot and press the F11 key.

3. Select 3-D Column as the graph format (the first option in the second row), and click Next to display the second dialog box.

4. Click Next again to move to the next dialog box, which was shown on page 82.

5. Accept the default settings and move to the fourth dialog box by clicking Next. (At any point in the graph-creating process, you can click the Back button to move back to a previous dialog box so that you can change these settings.)

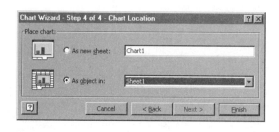

6. Here, the Chart Wizard asks where you want the graph to be displayed. With the As Object In Sheet1 setting selected, click Finish. Graph plots the graph and displays the Chart toolbar, as shown here (your toolbar may not be floating):

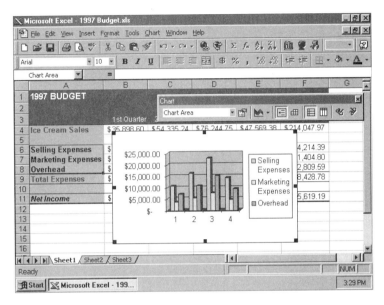

As you can see, four groups of columns represent the four quarters of expense data. Within each group, three colors represent the three expense categories, which are identified in the legend by the three labels from column A of the selected range: Selling Expenses, Marketing Expenses, and Overhead.

7. Turn off the Chart toolbar.

Sizing and Moving Graphs

When Graph finishes creating a graph and places it on a worksheet, it rarely places it where we want it to be. But moving and sizing graphs is easy, and we can always drag the graph to the desired location and then adjust its size by dragging small black squares, called *handles*, around the graph's frame. Try this:

Handles

1. Move the mouse pointer near the outer edge of the graph and when a pop-up box that says *Chart Area* appears, hold down the left mouse button and drag the graph approximately two

Chart Tips →

rows beneath the budget. (The handy pop-up boxes that identify different elements of the graph are called *Chart Tips*.)

Now try resizing the graph:

1. Point to the handle in the middle of the right side of the frame and drag it to the right. Graph redraws the graph within a wider frame.

Changing the height and width proportionally →

2. Drag a corner handle diagonally outward to increase both the height and the width proportionally.

3. When you've finished experimenting, reshape the graph so that it occupies an area of the worksheet about 16 rows high by 6 columns wide.

Updating Graphs

Excel has actively linked the graph to its underlying data, so if we change the data, Graph automatically redraws the graph to reflect the change. Try this:

1. Scroll upward, select cell E4 on the worksheet, and reenter the 4th Quarter sales as *98471.09*. The formulas go to work, producing drastic changes in the expenses and net income.

2. Use the scroll bar to bring this modified graph into view:

Adding values to an existing series

If you add values to a set of data in your worksheet and want to update a graph you created earlier to reflect the new values, you can select the values and simply drag the selection to the graph. When you release the mouse button, Excel adds the additional data points along the category axis. To add values to a graph located on a separate chart sheet, you can select the values, click the Copy button, move to the chart sheet, select the graph, and click the Paste button.

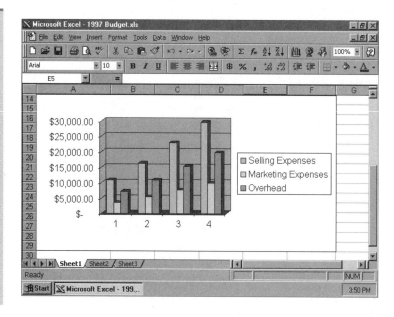

3. Click the Undo button to restore the original 4th Quarter amount.

Changing the Graph Type

Now that we've covered the basics of graph building, let's plot a new graph from the quarterly sales data so that we can explore the many available graphing possibilities. We will start by deleting the current graph and creating a new one:

1. Click the chart area to select the graph and press the Delete key. Excel removes the graph from the worksheet. ◄ Deleting graphs

2. Press Ctrl+Home and select A3:E4. The first row in this range contains labels that identify the four quarters of the budget year, and the second row contains numeric sales data.

3. Click the Chart Wizard button and click Finish to accept all the default settings in the four Chart Wizard dialog boxes. ◄ Creating a default graph

4. After Graph draws the graph, move and resize it as shown below:

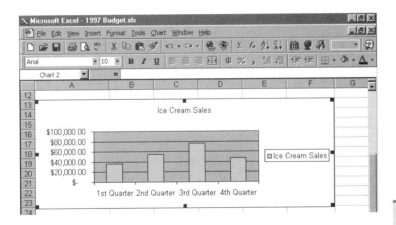

5. To change this column graph to a pie graph, be sure the graph is selected (surrounded by handles). If it isn't, click anywhere within the chart area to select it. Note that when the graph is selected, the Microsoft Graph program modifies the menus on the menu bar to accommodate the commands appropriate for working with graphs.

Graph scale

If you change the source data radically, the scale of the entire graph might change. For example, if you enter an ice cream sales amount in the millions in 1997 Budget, the other columns shrink down to almost nothing to keep the scale consistent.

6. Choose Chart Type from the Chart menu to display the dialog box shown here:

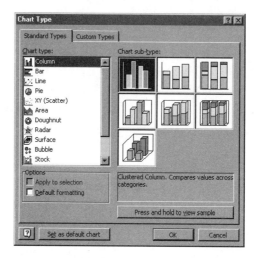

7. In the Chart Type list, select the Pie option and click OK. Graph draws this graph in which the four quarters of sales data are represented as colored wedges in a circular pie:

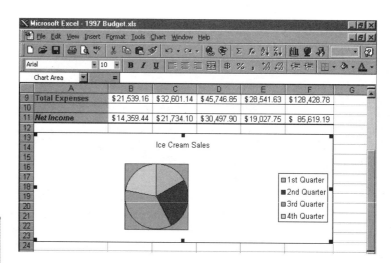

Selecting graph objects

If you find selecting a graph object with the mouse difficult, you can select the object from the Chart Objects list at the left end of the Chart toolbar. Graph then places handles around the object so that you can format it in the usual way.

8. Use Chart Tips to examine the value and percentage of each slice of the pie.

Before taking a look at some of the other available types, let's simplify things a bit by enlisting the aid of the Chart toolbar. Then we'll add another set of data—the net income amounts—to the graph. Follow these steps:

1. Choose Toolbars from the View menu and select Chart from the submenu to display the Chart toolbar. (You can move floating toolbars out of the way by dragging their title bars, or you can "dock" them at the top of the window by double-clicking their title bars.)

Displaying toolbars

2. Now click the arrow next to the Chart Type button on the Chart toolbar to display this drop-down palette of graph types:

The Chart Type button

3. Click the Column Chart option (the third option in the first column) to restore the previous chart type.

4. Next click anywhere outside the graph to deselect it, select A11:E11 in the budget worksheet, and click the Copy button.

Adding a set of data to a graph

5. Click one of the data markers (the graph's columns) and choose Paste Special from the Edit menu to display this dialog box:

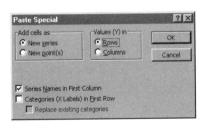

6. The default settings are correct, so click OK. Excel adds a second series of data markers to the graph, as shown on the next page.

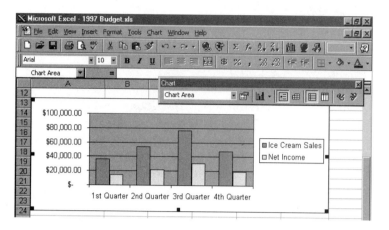

We can now compare sales with after-expenses income for each of the four quarters.

No matter what type of graph we need—bar, pie, line, and so on—Graph has a format that will probably do the job. The available types include:

Column graphs

- Column graphs (the default format), which are ideal for showing the variations in the value of an item over time, as with the budget example. In addition to the simple column graph that we've already created, we can plot stacked or 100-percent stacked column graphs; see the sub-types in the Chart Type dialog box shown on page 96.

Bar graphs

- Bar graphs, which are ideal for showing the variations in the value of an item over time, or for showing the values of several items at a single point in time.

Line graphs

- Line graphs, which are often used to show variations in the value of more than one item over time.

Area graphs

- Area graphs, which look something like line graphs but which plot multiple data series as cumulative layers with different colors, patterns, or shades.

Pie graphs

- Pie graphs, which are ideal for showing the percentages of an item that can be assigned to the item's components. (Pie graphs can represent only one data series.)

- Doughnut graphs, which display the data in a doughnut shape. Similar to the pie graph, they can, however, display more than one data series.

Doughnut graphs

- XY (or scatter) graphs, which are used to detect correlations between independent items (such as a person's height and weight).

XY graphs

- Radar graphs, which plot each series on its own axes radiating from a center point.

Radar graphs

- High-low-close graphs, which are typically used to plot stock-market activity.

High-low-close graphs

In addition, we can create three-dimensional area, bar, column, line, pie, and surface graphs. And we can create various kinds of combination graphs, which plot one type of graph on top of another as an "overlay." Each type has several variations that will satisfy most of our graphing needs. Let's try changing the type of the graph currently on the screen so that you can see some of the possibilities:

3-D graphs

Combination graphs

1. Be sure the graph is selected. Then click the arrow to the right of the Chart Type button on the Chart toolbar and click the Line Chart button in the left column of the drop-down palette. Sales and net income are now represented as two separate lines on the graph as shown here:

The Line Chart button

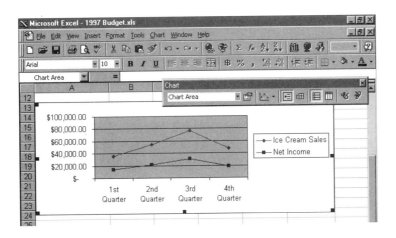

The 3-D Pie Chart button

2. Display the Chart Type drop-down palette and click the 3-D Pie Chart button. Now the four quarters of sales data are represented as colored wedges in a circular pie with the illusion of three dimensions. You no longer see the net income data because a pie graph can display only one set of data:

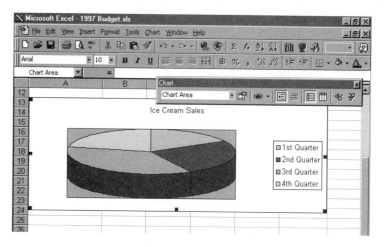

The Doughnut Chart button

3. Finally, click the Doughnut Chart button in the Chart Type button's palette. The resulting graph displays two circles, one for each type of data:

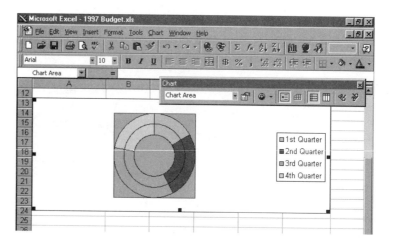

4. Click the other buttons in the Chart Type palette to get an idea of what's available. Finish up by clicking the Column Chart button to restore the two-dimensional column graph.

Using Graph Custom Types

Often, clicking one of the buttons in the Chart Type palette (or selecting one of the options in the Chart Type dialog box) will produce exactly the graph we need, but occasionally we might want something slightly different. Before we spend time adjusting the format of a graph type, we should check out the subtypes displayed on the Custom Types tab of the Chart Type dialog box. Follow these steps:

1. With the graph selected, choose Chart Type from the Chart menu and click the Custom Types tab to display the options shown here:

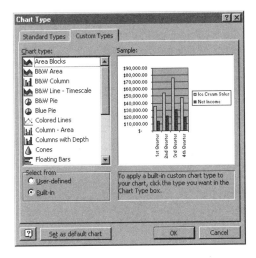

2. Scroll through the list, clicking any Chart Type options that catch your eye and noting their effect in the Sample box to the right.

3. When you've finished exploring, select Line-Column and click OK. The result—an example of a combination graph—is shown on the next page.

X-axis and y-axis

Graph uses the terms x-axis and y-axis with some of its graph commands. For clarification, here are a couple of definitions: The x-axis shows the information categories—for example, sales and expenses; the y-axis shows the data points (plotted values).

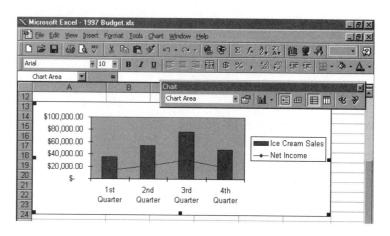

Fine-Tuning Graphs

As we have said, Graph has a graph type for almost every occasion. But often we will want to refine the presentation of a graph by adding or changing specific elements. For this purpose, Graph provides a wealth of options for fine-tuning graphs. We'll use some of these options to add a title, adjust the value-axis labels, add a frame, and change gridlines. These elements increase almost any graph's clarity and persuasiveness.

We can use commands on the menu bar to change the various elements of a graph; however, Graph provides object menus to make the job of customizing even easier. Object menus exist for almost every conceivable graph element. You might want to get a feel for the range of customization possibilities by right-clicking various graph elements (gridlines, axes, series, and so on) to open their object menus. When you've finished experimenting on your own, we'll show you how to add a title to the graph currently on your screen.

Displaying a data table

If you create a column, bar, line, or area graph on its own chart sheet or if the data used to plot the graph is not easy to spot on the worksheet, you can display a data table below the graph. Simply click the graph to select it, choose Chart Options from the Chart menu, and click the Data Table tab. Click the Show Data Table option and then click OK. If you want, you can add legend keys to the data table and delete the legend. To hide a data table, simply deselect the Show Data Table option.

Adding and Formatting Text

To dress up the graph, we can add a title with a subtitle and explanatory notes. (Titles appear at the top of the graph; notes can be placed anywhere on the graph. See the tip on the facing page.) We can also customize the axis labels. All the fonts and attributes available for worksheet entries are available for graph text, so we can format the text any way we want. Follow these steps to add a title to the graph:

1. With the graph selected, use Chart Tips to make sure you're in the chart area and then right-click. Choose Chart Options from the object menu and click the Titles tab to display this dialog box:

Adding a title

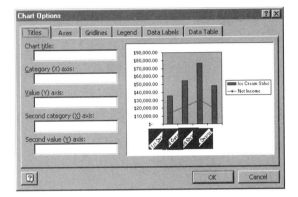

As you can see from the options, you can create a title and attach text to the axes.

2. Click an insertion point in the Chart Title edit box, type *1997 Budget*, and click OK.

3. Now click an insertion point at the end of the title, press Enter, and type *Ice Cream Sales and Net Income*. Then click anywhere on the graph to complete entry of the title, which now looks like this:

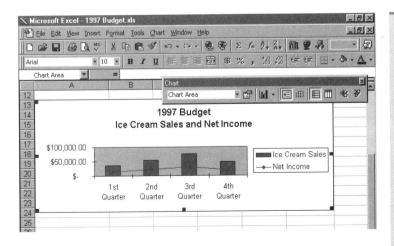

Adding notes

To add explanatory notes to a graph, check that no graph element is selected, click an insertion point in the formula bar, type the note, and press Enter. Excel displays a text box containing the note in the middle of the graph. You can use the frame and handles surrounding the text box to reposition it and resize it. To format the text box and the note it contains, right-click the box and make your selections in the Format Object dialog box.

Formatting the title

4. Right-click 1997 Budget to display the title's object menu. Then choose Format Chart Title and click the Font tab to display these options:

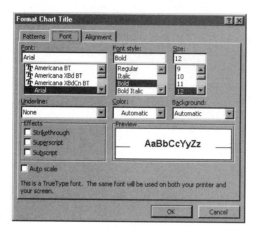

5. Select Times New Roman from the Font list, click Bold Italic in the Font Style list, and click OK.

Now let's make the default value-axis labels easier to read:

Formatting axis labels

1. Right-click the value-axis numbers, choose Format Axis from the object menu, and click the Number tab to display the dialog box shown on the facing page.

Creating graphics in Excel

With Excel's drawing tools, located on the Drawing toolbar, you can draw attention to specific parts of a graph or worksheet. (To display the Drawing toolbar, click the Drawing button on the Standard toolbar.) For example, you might circle a data point or mark it with an arrow. You can even create simple graphics, such as a logo. The best way to learn how to use the Line, Arrow, Rectangle, and Oval buttons is to experiment. To create a graphic object, click one of the buttons and drag it over the graph or worksheet. Holding down the Shift key as you drag constrains lines to 45-degree angles and creates perfect squares, circles, and arcs. When you release the mouse button, Excel surrounds the object with handles that you can use to reposition and resize the object. You can also use the AutoShapes button to create even more shapes, including FlowChart shapes. You use the various color and style buttons on the Drawing toolbar to adjust the object's line thickness, fill color, and pattern. To add free-floating notes to a graph or worksheet, click the Text Box button on the Drawing toolbar, drag out a box, and type the note. To add fancy-lettered text, use the Insert WordArt button.

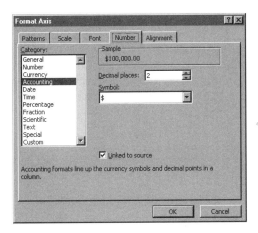

2. Select Currency in the Category list, change the Decimal Places setting to 0, and then click the Scale tab to display these options:

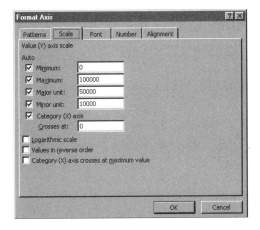

3. Under Auto, you can see that the value axis is scaled from 0 to 100,000, with a label at major-unit intervals of 50,000. Double-click the Major Unit edit box, type *20000* to display more labels along the value axis, and click OK. The results are shown on the next page.

Formatting legends

By default, Graph places the legend to the right of the plot area. If you want, you can move the legend to another part of the screen by simply dragging it. Alternatively, you can choose Format Legend from the legend's object menu and select an option on the Placement tab in the Format Legend dialog box. Other tabs in this dialog box allow you to change the pattern, color, and font of the legend.

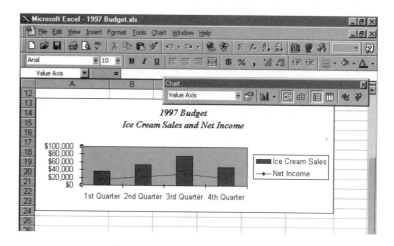

Enhancing the Graph's Border

We can use the Color and Font Color buttons on the Formatting toolbar to select colors and patterns for different elements of our graphs and worksheets. However, using the Format command on the object menu is the quickest way to customize the graph's border. Try this:

1. If necessary, select the graph. Then right-click the chart area and choose Format Chart Area from the object menu to display this dialog box:

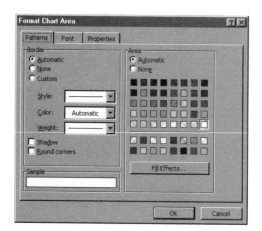

Formatting data markers

To change the color, pattern, or the legend name for a series of data markers, right-click one of the markers and then choose Format Data Series from the object menu. Graph displays a dialog box in which you can make these and other types of changes to the markers.

2. On the Patterns tab, click the arrow to the right of the Weight edit box in the Border section and select the third line. Click the Shadow option and then click OK.

We can also use this dialog box to give the graph's background a color or pattern.

Adding Gridlines

When gridlines would make it easier to read the plotted data, we can easily add them to a graph. We can also add lines for major or minor intervals on either or both axes. Our graph has gridlines for the value axis showing the dollar amounts. Let's add gridlines to the category axis:

1. With the graph selected, right-click any area of the graph, choose Chart Options from the object menu, and then click the Gridlines tab to display this dialog box:

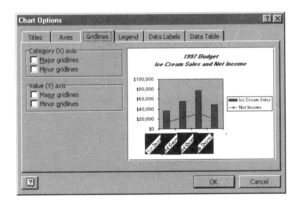

2. Click Major Gridlines in the Category [X] Axis section and then click OK. The graph now looks like this:

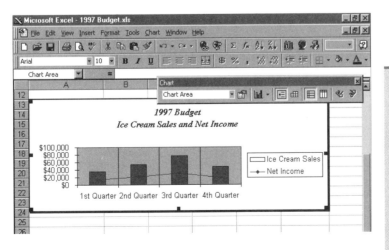

The SERIES function

If you click one of the bars in the graph, a SERIES function appears in the formula bar. This function links the graph to the source worksheet. Notice that the references are all absolute. If you change the position of the graphed data in the source worksheet, Graph will not be able to find the moved data.

3. Click anywhere on the worksheet to deselect the graph and remove the Chart toolbar. Then save the workbook before moving on.

We won't take our customization experiments any further but will leave you to explore on your own. When you're ready, rejoin us to print the graph.

Previewing and Printing Graphs

Previewing and printing graphs is much like previewing and printing worksheets. We can preview and print the worksheet data and graph together or just the graph. Follow these steps:

1. Press Ctrl+Home and then click the Print Preview button. Your screen now looks like this one:

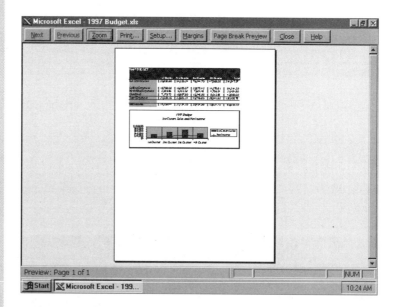

As you can see, one or two adjustments would greatly improve the look of this page.

2. Click the Close button to return to the worksheet. Then adjust the position of the graph so that it is separated from the worksheet entries by about five rows of blank cells.

3. Deselect the graph and click the Print Preview button again. Then click the Setup button on the Print Preview toolbar.

4. Click the Margins tab, change the Top margin to *1.5*, and in the Center On Page section, select the Horizontally option and then click OK. Here are the results:

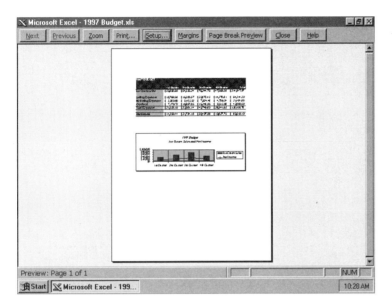

If you want, you can click the Print button on the Print Preview toolbar to create a paper copy of the graph.

Now that you are acquainted with Microsoft Graph and its customization options, you are well-equipped to produce professional-looking worksheets and to give your audiences alternative, easy-to-grasp ways of viewing your data.

Extracting Information
from a List

In Excel, a list is a simple database. Our examples show how to sort data and use powerful yet efficient tools to extract and manipulate information. We also experiment with filtering records, summarize data, and create a pivot table.

Sales Log.xls

Sum of Amount of Sale		Quarter				
Type	Product Name	1	2	3	4	Grand Total
Chain	Just Peachy	$1,399.07	$1,399.07	$1,399.07	$1,399.07	$5,596.28
	Kiwi Spree	$1,456.23	$1,456.23	$1,456.23	$1,456.23	$5,824.92
	Oh Fudge!	$5,175.66	$5,175.66	$5,175.66	$5,175.66	$20,702.64
	P B & J	$2,256.23	$2,256.23	$2,256.23	$2,256.23	$9,024.92
	Rootbeer Float	$2,068.30	$2,068.30	$2,068.30	$2,068.30	$8,273.20
	Thanks a Latte	$1,168.34	$1,168.34	$1,168.34	$1,168.34	$4,673.36
Chain Total		$13,523.83	$13,523.83	$13,523.83	$13,523.83	$54,095.32
Individual	Just Peachy	$345.00	$345.00	$345.00	$345.00	$1,380.00
	Kiwi Spree	$345.23	$345.23	$345.23	$345.23	$1,380.92
	Midnight Espresso	$1,532.46	$1,532.46	$1,532.46	$1,532.46	$6,129.84
	P B & J	$1,057.64	$1,057.64	$1,057.64	$1,057.64	$4,230.56
Individual Total		$3,280.33	$3,280.33	$3,280.33	$3,280.33	$13,121.32
Grand Total		$16,804.16	$16,804.16	$16,804.16	$16,804.16	$67,216.64

Create a pivot table to summarize worksheet data

Sales Log.xls

Sales Log
1997

Date	Quarter	Product Name	Customer Number	Type	Amount of Sale
1/3/97	1	Kiwi Spree	4739AA	Chain	$ 1,456.23
1/4/97	1	Midnight Espresso	943200	Individual	$ 875.56
1/10/97	1	Rootbeer Float	1488AA	Chain	$ 2,068.30
1/24/97	1	Just Peachy	6398AA	Chain	$ 1,399.07
2/2/97	1	Oh Fudge!	7945AA	Chain	$ 2,643.90
2/8/97	1	P B & J	825600	Individual	$ 1,057.64
2/14/97	1	Kiwi Spree	246500	Individual	$ 345.23
3/1/97	1	Thanks a Latte	5409AA	Chain	$ 1,168.34
3/11/97	1	P B & J	3867AA	Chain	$ 2,256.23
3/15/97	1	Midnight Espresso	975600	Individual	$ 656.90
3/20/97	1	Just Peachy	479300	Individual	$ 345.00
3/28/97	1	Oh Fudge!	6563AA	Chain	$ 2,531.76
4/3/97	2	Kiwi Spree	4739AA	Chain	$ 1,456.23
4/11/97	2	Midnight Espresso	943200	Individual	$ 875.56
4/19/97	2	Rootbeer Float	1488AA	Chain	$ 2,068.30
4/27/97	2	Just Peachy	6398AA	Chain	$ 1,399.07
5/5/97	2	Oh Fudge!	7945AA	Chain	$ 2,643.90
5/13/97	2	P B & J	825600	Individual	$ 1,057.64
5/21/97	2	Kiwi Spree	246500	Individual	$ 345.23
5/29/97	2	Thanks a Latte	5409AA	Chain	$ 1,168.34
6/6/97	2	P B & J	3867AA	Chain	$ 2,256.23
6/14/97	2	Midnight Espresso	975600	Individual	$ 656.90
6/22/97	2	Just Peachy	479300	Individual	$ 345.00
6/30/97	2	Oh Fudge!	6563AA	Chain	$ 2,531.76
7/3/97	3	Kiwi Spree	4739AA	Chain	$ 1,456.23
7/11/97	3	Midnight Espresso	943200	Individual	$ 875.56
7/19/97	3	Rootbeer Float	1488AA	Chain	$ 2,068.30
7/27/97	3	Just Peachy	6398AA	Chain	$ 1,399.07
8/4/97	3	Oh Fudge!	7945AA	Chain	$ 2,643.90
8/12/97	3	P B & J	825600	Individual	$ 1,057.64
8/20/97	3	Kiwi Spree	246500	Individual	$ 345.23
8/28/97	3	Thanks a Latte	5409AA	Chain	$ 1,168.34
9/5/97	3	P B & J	3867AA	Chain	$ 2,256.23
9/13/97	3	Midnight Espresso	975600	Individual	$ 656.90
9/21/97	3	Just Peachy	479300	Individual	$ 345.00
9/29/97	3	Oh Fudge!	6563AA	Chain	$ 2,531.76
10/2/97	4	Kiwi Spree	4739AA	Chain	$ 1,456.23
10/10/97	4	Midnight Espresso	943200	Individual	$ 875.56
10/18/97	4	Rootbeer Float	1488AA	Chain	$ 2,068.30
10/26/97	4	Just Peachy	6398AA	Chain	$ 1,399.07
11/3/97	4	Oh Fudge!	7945AA	Chain	$ 2,643.90
11/11/97	4	P B & J	825600	Individual	$ 1,057.64
11/19/97	4	Kiwi Spree	246500	Individual	$ 345.23
11/27/97	4	Thanks a Latte	5409AA	Chain	$ 1,168.34
12/5/97	4	P B & J	3867AA	Chain	$ 2,256.23

Sort the data for easier analysis

Create a series of evenly spaced dates

The data in these columns is summarized in the pivot table

Relational vs. flat databases

An Excel list is a flat database, meaning that it consists of one stand-alone table. You can sort the list, pull out specific records, and otherwise manipulate it, but you can work only with the data stored in that one table. A relational database consists of several tables that are linked by key fields. Suppose a database for Cream of the Crop consists of one table for sales-rep information, another for customer information, another for inventory, and another for invoices. Each sales rep, customer, product, and invoice is identified by a unique code in their respective tables' key fields that can be used in one table as a link to information in another table. For example, the invoice table could contain these fields: Invoice# (this table's key field), Customer# (the key field of the customer table), Rep # (the key field of the sales-rep table), Product # (the key field of the inventory table), Quantity, Unit Price, Amount, Delivery, Tax, and Total. For each record, an invoice could be generated that uses the key fields to pull the customer's billing, shipping, tax status, and delivery-cost information from the customer table; the sales rep's name and phone number from the sales-rep table; and the product's name, availability, and unit price from the inventory table. This type of power is beyond the capabilities of Excel but is a breeze for database programs like Microsoft Access.

We've covered a lot of important ground, and you now have a feel for some of the power of Excel. In this chapter, we show you more techniques for efficient worksheet creation and management. Using a sales log as a base worksheet, we describe how to sort and extract data and how to calculate statistics from a database, or *list*. If we have a database program, such as Microsoft Access, we'll probably want to perform these tasks using that program's more sophisticated database tools. But if our data is relatively straightforward, we can carry out many database tasks with Excel.

Let's start by creating the sales log for this example, and then we'll get down to business.

Cloning Worksheets

Using one worksheet as the basis for another is a very important time-saving technique. In this section, we will clone the Quarterly sheet of the 1997 Sales workbook to create a worksheet in another workbook called Sales Log. Then we'll use a few tricks to transform the new worksheet into a simulated sales log (a record of sales) to give us a large worksheet to manipulate in this chapter. If you need to create such a log for your work, you will obviously enter real data. Follow these steps to create Sales Log:

1. With Excel loaded, click the Open button to display the Open dialog box shown on page 28. Double-click 1997 Sales, which should be located in the My Documents folder, to open the 1997 Sales workbook.

2. Choose Save As from the File menu, and when the Save As dialog box appears, type *Sales Log* in the File Name edit box and click Save. You now have two identical workbooks saved under different names.

A few alterations to Sales Log will give us a usable worksheet with enough data for demonstration purposes. Remember to save your work frequently as you follow the steps in the next sections.

1. In cell A1 of the Quarterly sheet, type *Sales Log* and press Enter to enter the text in A1 and move down one cell. In cell A2, type *'1997* and then press Enter.

2. Select the headers for rows 4 through 12, right-click them to display the row object menu, and then choose Delete to remove the selected rows.

3. Select A5:F16, click the Copy button, click cell A17, and click the Paste button to insert the selected range of data.

4. Select A5:F28, click the Copy button, click cell A29, and click the Paste button to insert the selected range of data. Your worksheet now contains 48 rows of information.

Now, so that the log includes sales for all the months of the year, follow these steps:

1. Select cell A17, type *4/3/97*, and click the Enter button. Excel displays the new date for this sale and then recalculates the formula in cell B17, assigning the sale to the second quarter of the year instead of the first.

Rather than changing dates manually for the rest of the worksheet, we'll take this opportunity to demonstrate the Fill/Series command on the Edit menu. In a moment, we'll use this command to create a sequential set of numbers. Here, we'll use it to create a set of evenly spaced dates. (Obviously, if you were logging real sales in this database, you would use the actual sale dates.)

← Creating a series of evenly spaced dates

2. Select A17:A28 and choose Fill and then Series from the Edit menu. Excel displays this dialog box:

Automatic date series

You can use AutoFill to create a series of dates. Simply enter the starting date and drag the fill handle through the range you want to fill. Excel assumes you want to create a series with a step value of one day. To fill a range with the same date, without creating a series, hold down the Ctrl key while dragging the fill handle.

3. Because the value in cell A17 is a date, Excel assumes you want to create a set of dates. Type *8* in the Step Value box and then click OK. Excel uses the value in cell A17 as its starting point and creates a series of dates that are eight days apart. (To create a series that skips to Monday if a date falls on Saturday or Sunday, click the Weekday option before clicking OK.)

4. Select cell A29, type *7/3/97*, and click the Enter button.

Repeating a command → 5. Select A29:A40 and choose Repeat Series from the top of the Edit menu.

6. Select cell A41, type *10/2/97*, and click the Enter button.

7. Select A41:A52 and choose Repeat Series from the Edit menu.

8. Press Ctrl+Home and then scroll through the worksheet. The formulas in column B have done their work and assigned the sales to quarters based on the dates in column A.

This large worksheet is ideal for demonstrating some of Excel's list capabilities.

Sorting Data

The sales data in the 1997 Sales worksheet we created in PART ONE is not much larger than one screen. To find out which chain-store customer has purchased the most ice cream, we could simply look at the worksheet. Getting that information from the Sales Log worksheet is a little more difficult. Fortunately, Excel can quickly sort worksheets like this one, using one, two, or more levels of sorting.

Adding Sort Codes

Before we sort any large worksheet, we should ask ourselves whether we might need to put the data back in its original order. If there is even a chance that we will, we should add sort codes to the worksheet before we begin sorting. A *sort code* is a sequential number assigned to each row of entries. After changing the order of the entries, we can sort again on the basis of the sort code to put everything back where it was. Follow these steps to add sort codes to the sales log:

1. Select cell A3, right-click it to display the column object menu, and choose Insert to display the Insert dialog box. Select Entire Column and click OK.

2. Select cell A4, type *Sort Code*, and press Enter.

3. In cell A5, type *1* and press Enter. Then type *2* in cell A6 and press Enter.

Creating a series of numbers

4. Select A5:A6 and drag the fill handle in the bottom right corner of the selection down to cell A52. Excel uses the default settings of the Fill/Series command—Columns as the Series In option, Linear as the Type option, and a Step Value of 1—to produce a sequential set of numbers in the selected range, as shown here:

	A	B	C	D	E	F	G
4	Sort Code	Date	Quarter	Product Name	Customer Number	Type	Amount of Sale
5	1	1/3/97	1	Kiwi Spree	4739AA	Chain	$ 1,456.23
6	2	1/4/97	1	Midnight Espresso	943200	Individual	$ 875.56
7	3	1/10/97	1	Rootbeer Float	1488AA	Chain	$ 2,068.30
8	4	1/24/97	1	Just Peachy	6398AA	Chain	$ 1,399.07
9	5	2/2/97	1	Oh Fudge!	7945AA	Chain	$ 2,643.90
10	6	2/8/97	1	P B & J	825600	Individual	$ 1,057.64
11	7	2/14/97	1	Kiwi Spree	246500	Individual	$ 345.23
12	8	3/1/97	1	Thanks a Latte	5409AA	Chain	$ 1,168.34
13	9	3/11/97	1	P B & J	3867AA	Chain	$ 2,256.23
14	10	3/15/97	1	Midnight Espresso	975600	Individual	$ 656.90
15	11	3/20/97	1	Just Peachy	479300	Individual	$ 345.00
16	12	3/28/97	1	Oh Fudge!	6563AA	Chain	$ 2,531.76
17	13	4/3/97	2	Kiwi Spree	4739AA	Chain	$ 1,456.23
18	14	4/11/97	2	Midnight Espresso	943200	Individual	$ 875.56
19	15	4/19/97	2	Rootbeer Float	1488AA	Chain	$ 2,068.30

Now let's look at various ways we might want to sort the Quarterly sheet of the Sales Log workbook.

Using One Sort Column

The simplest sorting procedure is based on only one column. We indicate which column Excel should use, and the program

A step value other than 1

To use AutoFill to create a series with a step value other than 1, enter the first and second values in the series, select both values, and drag the fill handle through the range in which you want the series to appear. The second value tells Excel what to use as a step value. For example, entering 1 and 4 tells Excel to create a series with a step value of 3—the difference between 1 and 4. (To create a series of numbers using Auto-Fill, you must enter two values; if you enter only one, Excel simply fills the range with the starting value.)

rearranges the rows of the selected range accordingly. Let's start by sorting the data in Sales Log by customer type to see how the process works:

1. Select A5:G52. (If A5:A52 is already selected, you can hold down Shift and press the Right Arrow key six times to quickly extend the selection.)

2. Choose Sort from the Data menu. Excel displays the Sort dialog box:

You can select three different columns for sorting. Excel automatically enters the first column in the selection in the Sort By edit box.

3. You want Excel to use the Type column as the basis for a one-column sort, so click the arrow to the right of the Sort By edit box to drop down a list of the columns in the selection. Click the bottom scroll arrow to scroll the list, and then select Type.

4. By default, Excel selects Ascending as the sort order for the records. Click OK to sort the records with the current settings.

The sales data is now sorted alphabetically by customer type, with all the sales to chain stores coming before those to individually-owned stores.

Using Two Sort Columns

Now let's take things a step further and sort the sales data not only by type but also by product name:

Sorting buttons

Two sorting buttons, located on the Standard toolbar, can be used when you are sorting data based on only one column. Tell Excel which column is the sort column by clicking a cell in that column before using the sorting button. Then click the Sort Ascending button to sort the list starting with A (or lowest digit) or the Sort Descending button to sort starting with Z (or highest digit). Excel then sorts the list in which the cell you selected is located. To restore the data to its original order, use the Undo button on the Standard toolbar.

1. With the range still highlighted, choose Sort from the Data menu. The previous sort column, Type, is still entered in the Sort By edit box.

2. To add a second sort column, click the arrow to the right of the first Then By edit box, select Product Name, and click OK.

   The sales log is now sorted alphabetically by customer type and alphabetically within type by the product names of the ice cream.

Using Three Sort Columns

Depending on the focus of our current analysis, we might want to sort Sales Log based on the Date or Quarter columns. However, let's assume we are interested in the sales volume of each product and add one more column to the sort. Let's sort by customer type, product name, and amount of sale:

1. With A5:G52 still selected, choose Sort from the Data menu. Again, the Sort dialog box retains the selections from the previous sort.

2. Click the arrow to the right of the second Then By edit box, select Amount of Sale, and click OK.

3. Press Ctrl+Home to see these results (we've scrolled the screen a little):

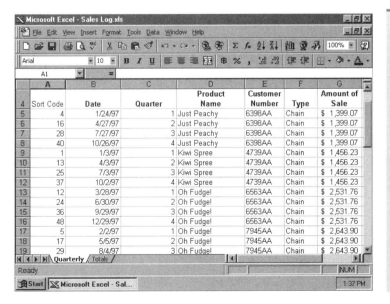

Sorting by columns

If your list has field names down the leftmost column instead of across the top row and your data is oriented horizontally instead of vertically, you will want to sort by columns instead of rows. Select the list (but not the field names) and in the Sort dialog box, click the Options button to display the Sort Options dialog box. Then in the Orientation section, select Sort Left To Right and click OK. Select the Sort By options you want in the Sort dialog box and then click OK to sort the data.

Keeping Headings in View

We can now scroll through the sales log to check how Excel has sorted the data, but as we scroll, the column headings will scroll out of sight. We can keep the headings at the top of the screen like this:

1. If necessary, scroll the worksheet so that row 4—the row with the column headings—is at the top of your screen.

Splitting the window into panes

2. Select cell A5 and choose Split from the Window menu to position a horizontal split bar across the worksheet window above the selected cell, like this:

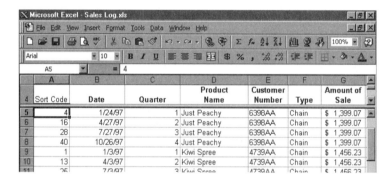

If you select any cell in row 1 (except A1) and choose Split, Excel positions a vertical split bar down the worksheet window to the left of the selected cell. If you select a single cell that is not in row 1 or column A and then choose Split, Excel splits the window horizontally and vertically above and to the left of the selected cell.

Synchronized scrolling

If you split the worksheet window horizontally and then use the horizontal scroll bar to scroll the window, both panes of the window scroll so that columns always align. Likewise, if you split the worksheet window vertically and then use the vertical scroll bar, the rows scroll simultaneously.

3. Use the scroll bar for the lower windowpane to scroll the sorted data while the column headings remain visible in the upper windowpane.

4. When you finish viewing the data, restore the single pane by choosing Remove Split from the Window menu.

List Basics

The sales log is an organized collection of information about ice cream sales. By common definition, it is a *database*, known in Excel as a *list*. A list is a table of related data with a rigid structure that enables you to easily locate and evaluate individual items of information. Each row of a list is a *record* that contains all the pertinent information about one component of the list. For example, row 5 of the sales log contains all the information about one particular sale. Each cell of the list is a *field* that contains one item of information. Cell G5, for example, contains the amount of sale for the record in row 5. All the fields in a particular column contain the same kind of information about their respective records. For example, column B of the sales log contains the dates of all the sales. At the top of each column is a heading, called a *field name*.

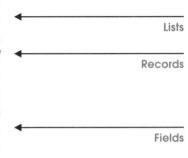

Lists

Records

Fields

In the next sections, we'll cover Excel's list capabilities. First, however, follow these steps to restore the sales log to its original order and to make a few other necessary adjustments:

1. Select A5:G52 and choose Sort from the Data menu to display the Sort dialog box. Click the arrow to the right of the Sort By edit box and then select Sort Code. For each of the two Then By edit boxes, click their arrows and select (none) from their drop-down lists. Click OK. Excel sorts the records back into their original order.

2. Right-click the column A header to display the column object menu and choose Delete. The sales log now contains only its original six columns.

We are now ready to begin exploring Excel's list operations, which we perform with the aid of a dialog box called a *data form*. As you'll see in the following sections, the options in the data form provide ways to find, add, delete, and modify records. Complete these steps to display the data form:

1. Select the first cell of the list—in this case, cell A5.

2. Choose Form from the Data menu. The data form shown on the next page appears.

Freezing panes

You can use Freeze Panes on the Window menu to lock rows, columns, or both so that you can then keep column or row headings in view while you scroll other portions of the worksheet. To freeze a row or rows, select the row above which you want to make the freeze and choose Freeze Panes from the Window menu. Similarly, to freeze a column or columns, select the column to the right of which you want to make the freeze and then choose the command. Selecting a single cell and then choosing the command freezes the rows above and columns to the left of the selected cell. Choose Unfreeze Panes to return the panes to their original condition.

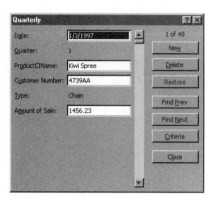

As you can see, the name of the sheet appears in the title bar of the dialog box. The column headings have become the field names and are displayed down the left side of the form. One record's data is displayed in the edit boxes adjacent to the field names. If a field contains a formula, as the Quarter field does, the data form displays the results of the formula, not the formula itself. The result is not in an edit box, indicating that we can't edit the field.

Finding Records

The data form allows us to find records by stepping through the list one record at a time or by entering criteria to identify specific records. Let's step through the list first:

1. Click the Find Next button in the data form. Excel displays the second record. The numbers in the top right corner show how many records are in the list and which record is currently displayed.

Data form size

Excel can display up to 32 fields on a data form. If your list has over 32 fields, when you choose Form from the Data menu to display a data form, Excel tells you that your list has too many fields. Reduce the number of fields and try again. (A quick way to reduce the number of fields without losing data is to insert a blank column after the 32nd field.)

2. Click the Find Prev and Find Next buttons to step back and forth through the list. When you are finished, use the scroll bar to the right of the fields to return to record 1.

We use the Criteria button in the data form to find a specific record or records in the list, like this:

1. Click the Criteria button to display the criteria form, which resembles a blank data form.

2. To find all sales over $2,000 for P B & J, type *P B & J* in the
Product Name edit box and *>2000* in the Amount of Sale edit
box, as shown here:

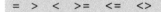
Entering criteria

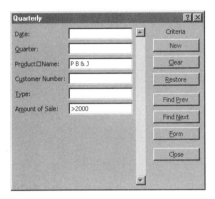

3. Click the Find Next button. Excel moves you back to the data
form, where the first record in the list that meets the criteria
is displayed. Click the Find Next button again, and Excel
displays the next record that meets the criteria. You can
continue clicking the Find Next button until you reach the end
of the list. Then move back through the matching records by
clicking the Find Prev button.

4. Return to the criteria form by clicking the Criteria button and
then remove the criteria by clicking the Clear button.

5. Move back to the data form by clicking the Form button. All
records are now accessible.

Adding and Deleting Records

The data form can be used to add and delete records from the
list. As an example, we'll add a new record, find it, and then
remove it from the list. Follow these steps:

1. With the data form displayed on your screen, click the New
button. Excel clears the fields of the data form so that you can
type the information for a new record. New Record is displayed in the top right corner.

Comparison operators and wildcards

You can use these comparison operators to compute criteria:

= > < >= <= <>

and you can specify wildcards,
using an * or a ? for matching text.
For example, assuming another
ice cream product named *Kiwi
Jubilee* has been added to the list,
you could specify *Kiwi** as the
Product Name to locate the records for both Kiwi Spree and
Kiwi Jubilee.

2. Fill in the record with the following data, using the Tab key to move from field to field:

Date	*11/4/97*
Product Name	*Rootbeer Float*
Customer Number	*4980AA*
Amount of Sale	*1595*

Because Quarter and Type are calculated fields, you don't need to enter anything for those fields. The data form now looks like this:

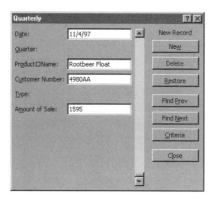

3. Click the New button or press Enter to add the record to the sales log. (Excel adds new records to the end of a list.)

4. Click the Find Prev button. Excel displays the record you just added—record 49. Notice that the calculated fields now have data in them.

5. With the new record still displayed, click the Delete button. Excel warns you that the record will be permanently deleted.

6. Click OK. Excel deletes the record and displays the data form for a new record.

The Restore button

When you are editing a record in a data form, you can restore the previous data by clicking the Restore button. This button works only if you haven't yet moved to another record or pressed the Enter key.

7. Click the Find Prev button again. The last record in the list is again record 48.

8. Click Close to remove the data form from the screen and return to your worksheet.

Filtering Records

Suppose we have invested a considerable chunk of our advertising budget for the year on a direct-mail flyer about a two-week promotion. For another two-week promotion earlier in the year, we relied on our salespeople to get the word out to their customers. We want to compare sales during the two promotions. Or suppose we want to analyze all sales over $1,000 to see if we can detect sales patterns. In either case, we can tell Excel to extract all the relevant data for scrutiny. We give Excel instructions of this kind by choosing Filter and then AutoFilter from the Data menu and then defining filtering criteria. To see how AutoFilter works, follow these steps:

AutoFilter

1. With row 4 at the top of your screen and cell A5 selected, choose Filter and then AutoFilter from the Data menu. Excel displays arrow buttons for each field, like this:

	A	B	C	D	E	F	G
4	Date	Quarter	Product Name	Customer Numbe	Type	Amount of Sale	
5	1/3/97	1	Kiwi Spree	4739AA	Chain	$ 1,456.23	
6	1/4/97	1	Midnight Espresso	943200	Individual	$ 875.56	
7	1/10/97	1	Rootbeer Float	1488AA	Chain	$ 2,068.30	
8	1/24/97	1	Just Peachy	6398AA	Chain	$ 1,399.07	
9	2/2/97	1	Oh Fudge!	7945AA	Chain	$ 2,643.90	
10	2/8/97	1	P B & J	825600	Individual	$ 1,057.64	
11	2/14/97	1	Kiwi Spree	246500	Individual	$ 345.23	
12	3/1/97	1	Thanks a Latte	5409AA	Chain	$ 1,168.34	

2. Click the arrow for the Quarter field. Excel displays a list of the unique values in the Quarter field—1, 2, 3, and 4—as well as three other options—All, Top 10, and Custom.

3. Click the arrow for the Product Name field. Again, Excel displays a list of the unique names in the field and the three other options.

4. Select Just Peachy. Excel immediately filters out all the records for Just Peachy, hiding the other records as shown on the next page.

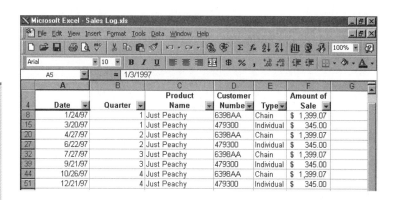

Advanced filtering

You can create a criteria range on your worksheet to use for more complex filtering. For example, if you want to find records over a certain amount for two products within a particular quarter, you start by creating a three-column-by-three-row table, called a *criteria range*, above the list. In the first row, enter the Quarter, Amount of Sale, and Product Name field names, spelling them exactly as they are in the list. (For filtering purposes, remove the line break from the Product Name field name in the list.) In the second row, enter the quarter number, sales amount (preceded by >, the greater than symbol), and name of the first product. In the third row, enter the quarter number, sales amount (preceded by >), and name of the second product. Then click any cell in the list and choose Filter and then Advanced Filter from the Data menu. Complete the dialog box by entering the references of both the list range and the criteria range (including both sets of field names), and click OK. Excel extracts the requested data from the list. (Choose Filter and then Show All from the Data menu to restore the list.) Using a criteria range is especially useful if you want to extract records based on calculated criteria, because you can use Excel's functions in the criteria formulas.

Notice that Excel retains the original record numbers and changes the color of the arrow for the Product Name field to indicate which column is being used for filtering.

Suppose we want to see the Just Peachy records for the second quarter only. Try this:

1. Click the down arrow for the Quarter field and select 2. Now only the second quarter records for Just Peachy are displayed.

2. To display all of the Just Peachy records again, click the down arrow for the Quarter field and select (All).

Customizing Filters

Now let's get a little fancy. Suppose we want to see only the records for Just Peachy with amounts over $1,000. To filter out these records, we use the Custom option on the drop-down list. Follow these steps:

1. Click the arrow for the Amount of Sale field and select (Custom...) to display this Custom AutoFilter dialog box:

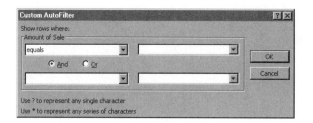

In this dialog box, you can use operators and the And or Or options to set criteria for the Amount of Sale field.

2. Click the arrow to the right of *equals* to display a list of operators, and then select *is greater than*.

← Using operators in filters

3. Press the Tab key to move to the adjacent criteria box, and type *1000*.

4. Click OK. Excel selects the records and displays these results:

We can remove all the filters we've set up so far by choosing Filter and then Show All from the Data menu. We can then apply different filters to the entire list. As another example, let's filter out the first and third quarter sales from the list by using the Or option in the Custom AutoFilter dialog box:

1. Choose Filter and then Show All from the Data menu. Excel displays all the records in the database.

2. Click the arrow for the Quarter field and select (Custom...).

3. In the Custom AutoFilter dialog box, leave *equals* as the operator and type *1* as the first criteria. Then click the Or option, select *equals* as the operator, and type *3* as the second criteria. The dialog box looks like the one on the next page.

Other AutoFilter options

When you select the Top 10 option from a column's drop-down list and set the Show options in the Top 10 AutoFilter dialog box, Excel sorts the rows based on the selected column and filters out the specified number of records at the top or bottom of the sorted list. For example, you can ask to see the eight records with the highest values in the Amount of Sale column.

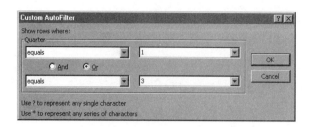

4. Click OK to display these results:

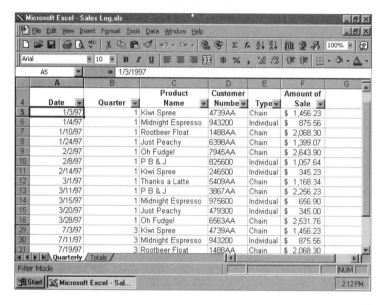

Turning off AutoFilter

5. Turn off filtering by choosing Filter from the Data menu and then choosing AutoFilter from the submenu to deactivate it. Excel displays all the records again.

Filtering enables us to act on only the filtered records, without affecting the other records in the database. For example, we can change the font of filtered records or sort them. We can also create a graph using the data from filtered records (see Chapter 4 for information about graphs).

Summarizing Data

Often we will want to summarize the data in a list in some way—for example, by totaling sets of entries. In Chapter 3, we summarized data by consolidating it (see page 78). Here, we'll look at another summarizing technique: *pivot tables*. Excel's PivotTable Wizard walks us through the steps of creating a pivot table with the type of summary calculation we specify. After we create the pivot table, we can reformat it by "pivoting" rows and columns on the screen to provide different views of the data.

The PivotTable Wizard

Let's use the sales log to build a pivot table, and then we'll modify the table. First display the PivotTable toolbar by following these steps:

1. Right-click anywhere on a toolbar to display the toolbar object menu, and choose PivotTable to display the PivotTable toolbar.

Displaying the PivotTable toolbar

2. If necessary, double-click the toolbar's title bar to "dock" the toolbar below the Formatting toolbar, like this:

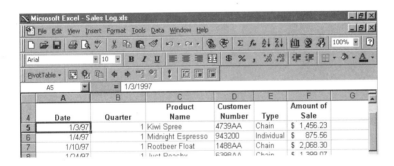

3. Take a moment to point to each button so that ToolTips can give you some idea of what the buttons do.

Creating a Pivot Table

We'll start by building a pivot table that summarizes the quarterly sales data for each product. Follow these steps:

1. Click the PivotTable Wizard button to display the first of its four dialog boxes as shown on the next page. (If necessary, close the Office Assistant.)

The PivotTable Wizard button

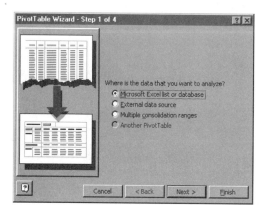

2. Click Next to create a pivot table from an Excel list. The wizard displays this Step 2 dialog box:

3. Ensure that the Range edit box contains an absolute reference to A4:F52 and then click Next to display the Step 3 dialog box, where you set up the pivot table layout by dragging the necessary fields (displayed as buttons on the right side of the dialog box) to the appropriate layout areas.

4. Drag the Product Name field button to the ROW area, drag the Quarter field button to the COLUMN area, and drag the Amount of Sale button to the DATA area, as shown below. (By default, Excel will calculate the sum of the Amount of Sale data.)

Microsoft Query

Excel ships with a program called Microsoft Query that you can use to access data in files that were created with database programs such as Paradox, dBASE, Microsoft Access, and Microsoft FoxPro. For more information, look up *Microsoft Query* in the Help Topics dialog box.

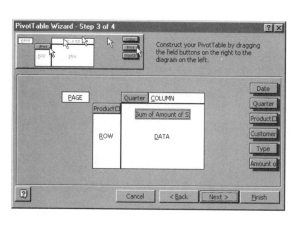

5. Click Next to display the Step 4 dialog box. Select the Existing Worksheet option, click the Collapse button to collapse the dialog box, and click cell H5. Then click the Expand button to redisplay the dialog box. Excel enters an absolute reference to cell H5 of the Quarterly sheet in the Existing Worksheet edit box, as shown here:

◄─────
Specifying the pivot table's
location

6. Click Finish and then scroll the screen to the right to see the new pivot table, which Excel has created in H5:M14:

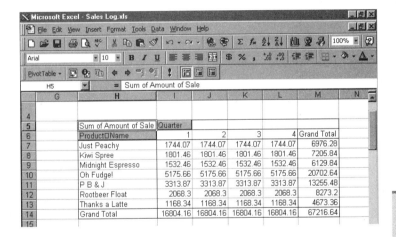

Excel has totaled the sales by product and by quarter, and has also calculated yearly totals for each product and quarterly totals for the entire product line.

Modifying a Pivot Table

Now that we have built a basic table, we can easily modify it with a variety of tools that Excel provides. Let's start by adding a field to the PAGE area of the table. The PAGE area allows

Naming lists

If you know you will add data to a list for which you are constructing a pivot table, assign a name to the entire list and enter that name in the Range edit box of the Step 2 dialog box. Then any data you add will be included in future versions of the pivot table (after you click the Refresh Data button on the PivotTable toolbar) without requiring that you go back and adjust the range.

us to filter the data in the table—for example, we can see only the Chain data or only the Individual data. Follow these steps:

1. With any cell in the pivot table selected, click the PivotTable Wizard button. Excel displays the Step 3 dialog box with the current pivot table's settings.

2. Drag the Type field button to the PAGE area and then click Finish.

3. Scroll the pivot table upward. Excel has added the Type field above the table, together with a filter—currently set to All—that allows you to view the data in different ways:

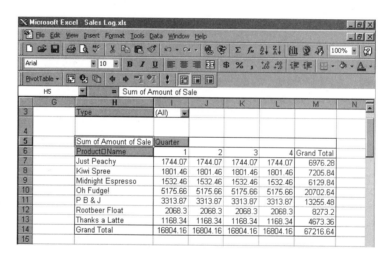

4. Click the filter's arrow and select Chain from the drop-down list to display the totals for only the chain stores. Repeat this step for the individually-owned stores, and then select All to redisplay the totals for both store types.

We can change the type of calculation for the Amount of Sale field by using either of two buttons: the PivotTable Wizard button or the PivotTable Field button. We'll use first one and then the other:

1. With any cell in the pivot table selected, click the PivotTable Wizard button to display the Wizard's Step 3 dialog box.

Updating pivot tables

If you change the data in a list that is the source for a pivot table, you can update the pivot table to reflect the new data by first clicking any cell in the pivot table and then clicking the Refresh Data button on the PivotTable toolbar or choosing the Refresh Data command from the Data menu.

2. Double-click Sum Of Amount Of Sale in the DATA area to display this dialog box:

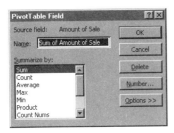

3. Select Count from the Summarize By list and click OK. The DATA area now indicates that Count Of Amount Of Sale is the calculation option.

4. Click Finish to return to the worksheet, where the pivot table now looks like this:

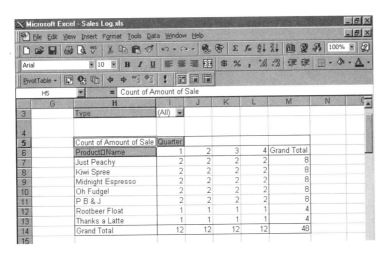

5. To total the sales amounts again, check that cell H5, Count Of Amount Of Sale, is selected and click the PivotTable Field button to display the PivotTable Field dialog box. Select Sum from the Summarize By list, but don't click OK yet.

The PivotTable Field button

6. To format the values in the pivot table, click the Number button to display the Format Cells dialog box, select the Currency category, and click OK twice. Excel totals the sales

Formatting a pivot table

by product and by quarter, displays the results in dollars and cents, and adjusts the column widths to accommodate the new values, as shown here:

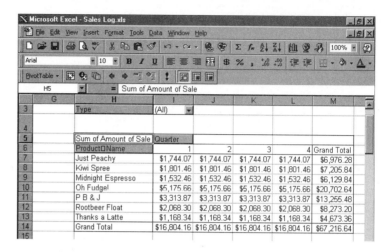

We can also manipulate the data by moving the fields on the worksheet. We can drag any field in the pivot table to any area to produce almost instantly any summarized format we choose. For example, suppose we want to see the total amount for each store type and for each product within each store type. We can combine the Type and Product Name fields in the ROW area, like this:

Moving fields

1. Point to cell H3 and drag the Type field down and to the left of cell H6, which contains the Product Name field. Excel calculates the data for both fields.

2. To display more of the pivot table, turn off the PivotTable toolbar by right-clicking any toolbar and then choosing Pivot-Table from the object menu. The results are shown on the facing page.

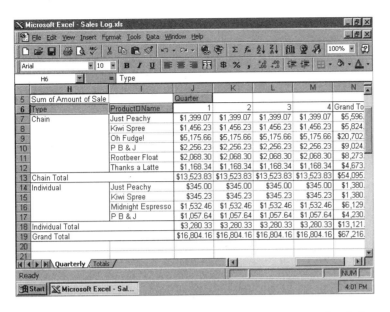

3. Press Ctrl+Home and click the Save button to save the Sales Log workbook.

In this chapter, we've only scratched the surface as far as pivot tables in particular and lists in general are concerned. As you use these features, you'll find that they can make light work of extraction and summarization, perhaps encouraging you to tackle tasks that would otherwise seem too intimidating, cumbersome, or time-consuming.

6 More Advanced Calculations

We build a set of worksheets and link them so that formulas in one worksheet can look up information in another. We also use iteration to project profit margin. Then we cover three types of what-if analysis: goal-seeking, data tables, and scenarios.

Resolve circular references with iteration

PROJECT COST ESTIMATE

Date 8/22/97	**Personnel Cost**	$ 9,688.00
Client Cream of the Crop	**Direct Expenses**	$ 1,050.00
Project Ad Campaign	**Total Cost**	$ 10,738.00
Estimate $ 16,520.00	**Profit Margin**	$ 5,782.00

Name	Hours	Hourly Rate	Billable Rate	Billable Total
Bole, Tye D.	40	$ 18.00	$ 35.00	$ 1,400.00
Boyardee, Jeff	80	$ 21.00	$ 38.00	$ 3,040.00
Butterworth, Missy	32	$ 15.00	$ 32.00	$ 1,024.00
Poe, Al	40	$ 25.00	$ 42.00	$ 1,680.00
Seltzer, Al K.	48	$ 36.00	$ 53.00	$ 2,544.00

Look up information in other workbooks

Current lease per month	$ 1,666.67		
Desired monthly payment	$ 2,200.00		
Price	$ (108,500.55)		
Interest	8%		
Term	60		
Payment	$2,200.00		

Interest	Payment
	$ 1,808.34
6.0%	$ 2,097.62
6.5%	$ 2,122.94
7.0%	$ 2,148.44
7.5%	$ 2,174.13
8.0%	$ 2,200.00
8.5%	$ 2,226.06

Use the Goal Seek command to find an unknown value

Months

	#DIV/0!	36	48	60
Interest	6.0%	$ 3,300.80	$ 2,548.14	$ 2,097.62
	6.5%	$ 3,325.43	$ 2,573.09	$ 2,122.94
	7.0%	$ 3,350.18	$ 2,598.18	$ 2,148.44
	7.5%	$ 3,375.04	$ 2,623.42	$ 2,174.13
	8.0%	$ 3,400.01	$ 2,648.82	$ 2,200.00
	8.5%	$ 3,425.10	$ 2,674.35	$ 2,226.06

Use data tables to calculate the effects of one or two variables

Scenario Summary

	Current Values:	Current Location	First Location	Second Location
Changing Cells:				
$B$9	35,000	35,000	43,000	48,000
$B$10	2,450	2,450	3,500	4,500
$B$11	20,000	20,000	21,000	27,500
$B$12	1,200	1,200	2,200	4,200
Result Cells:				
Over_Rate	17	17	18	19

Notes: Current Values column represents values of changing cells at time Scenario Summary Report was created. Changing cells for each scenario are highlighted in gray.

Create scenarios to evaluate the effect of changes

I n this chapter, we tackle a more ambitious set of worksheets and a more advanced set of calculations. First we create tables of employee information and overhead costs. Then we create a worksheet in another workbook that estimates project costs by "looking up" hourly rates in one of the tables. Next, we cover a technique called *iteration*, which enables Excel to resolve circular calculations. Finally, we explore some of Excel's tools for "what-if" analysis: the Goal Seek command, data tables, and Scenario Manager. For the exercises in this chapter, we'll develop worksheets for an advertising agency that wants to bid on a marketing project for the Cream of the Crop ice cream company.

Deciding what information you'll need ──────────▶

In our example, we create only employee information and overhead tables, because the primary cost involved in the marketing project estimate is for people's time. However, you can easily adapt the project estimate worksheet to incorporate other types of expenses. For example, if you manage a construction business that specializes in bathroom and kitchen remodeling, you can create a table with up-to-date prices for fixtures, plumbing supplies, cabinets, tile, and so on, in addition to the employee information and overhead tables. Even if you are a one-person operation with no employees, you can still adapt the worksheet to make sure that you include overhead and other costs in your project estimates.

This chapter differs from previous chapters in that we don't bog down the instructions with information you already know. For example, we might show you a worksheet and ask you to create it, without always telling you step by step what to enter, how to apply formats and styles, and how to adjust column widths. We leave it up to you to create the worksheet using the illustration as a guide. Similarly, we might tell you to create a formula, assuming that you know how to enter a function in a cell and how to click cells to use their references as arguments.

For this example, we'll organize the project information in two sheets, Employees and Overhead, saved within a single workbook. We'll also work with multiple workbooks and show you how to create links between them.

Creating the Supporting Tables

The logical way to begin this example is to enter the data needed for the two supporting tables. There's nothing complicated about these tables; we've stripped them down so that you don't have to type any extraneous information. The few calculations involved have been greatly simplified and do not reflect the gyrations accountants would go through to ensure to-the-penny accuracy. So instead of describing in detail how to create these tables, we'll simply show them to you and, after discussing the few formulas and cell and range names involved, let you create them on your own:

1. Open a new workbook, rename Sheet1 as *Employees*, and then save the workbook in the My Documents folder as *Costs*.

The Employee sheet

2. Create the following table of employee information:

	A	B	C	D	E	F	G	
1	EMPLOYEE INFORMATION							
2								
3	Name	Salary	Salary/Hour	Emp. Costs	Costs/Hour	Hourly Rate	Billable	
4	Bole, Tye D.	22000					y	
5	Boyardee, Jeff	26000					y	
6	Butterworth, Missy	19000					y	
7	Clean, M.R.	58000						
8	Key-Blurr, Ernie	23000					y	
9	Leigh, Sarah	40000					y	
10	Meyer, Oskar	32000					y	
11	Poe, Al	31000					y	
12	Seltzer, Al K.	44000					y	
13	Sin, Anna	67000						
14								
15								
16								

3. In row 4, enter these formulas:

C4   =B4/50/30
        Annual salary divided by 50 weeks (allowing 2 weeks for vacation), divided by 30 billable hours per week (allowing 2 hours per day of nonbillable time)

D4   =B4*.22
        Employer contributions to social security and benefits estimated at 22 percent of annual salary

Ascending order

You can list employees in the employee information table in any order, but before Excel can use the table to look up information, you must sort it in ascending order. Excel cannot look up information in randomly ordered tables or in tables in descending order. Select the range and use the Sort command on the Data menu to sort the table.

E4   =D4/52/30
                    Employer contributions to social security and
                    benefits divided by 52 weeks divided by 30 hours
                    per week

The ROUND function ──────▶ F4   =ROUND(C4+E4,0)
                    Salary per hour plus benefits per hour, rounded to
                    a whole number (0 decimal places)

4. After entering the formulas in row 4, select C4:F13 and choose Fill and then Down from the Edit menu to copy the row 4 formulas to rows 5 through 13.

5. Use the Comma Style and Decrease Decimal buttons on the Formatting toolbar to add commas and display no decimals in the amounts in columns B and D. Use the Decrease Decimal button to display two decimals in the amounts in columns C and E. Then adjust the column widths as needed to make the table more readable.

6. Choose Name and then Define from the Insert menu to assign the name *Billable* to cells G4:G14 and the name *Emp_Rate* to cells A4:F14. (See page 64 for information about how to assign range names.) We'll use these names in future formulas to create links between this and other worksheets. Press Ctrl+Home and save your work. Here is the completed table:

Extending named ranges

It is a good idea to always include a blank row or column at the end of a range when assigning range names. If you need to add employees to the Employees sheet, for example, you can select the blank row below the last entry and choose Rows from the Insert menu to add a new row. Because the blank row is part of the range named Billable, Excel automatically extends the range name definition to include the new row.

Microsoft Excel - Costs.xls

File Edit View Insert Format Tools Data Window Help

Arial | 10 | B I U | $ % , | A1 | = EMPLOYEE INFORMATION

	A	B	C	D	E	F	G
1	EMPLOYEE INFORMATION						
2							
3	Name	Salary	Salary/Hour	Emp. Costs	Costs/Hour	Hourly Rate	Billable
4	Bole, Tye D.	22,000	14.67	4,840	3.10	18	y
5	Boyardee, Jeff	26,000	17.33	5,720	3.67	21	y
6	Butterworth, Missy	19,000	12.67	4,180	2.68	15	y
7	Clean, M.R.	58,000	38.67	12,760	8.18	47	
8	Key-Blurr, Ernie	23,000	15.33	5,060	3.24	19	y
9	Leigh, Sarah	40,000	26.67	8,800	5.64	32	y
10	Meyer, Oskar	32,000	21.33	7,040	4.51	26	y
11	Poe, Al	31,000	20.67	6,820	4.37	25	y
12	Seltzer, Al K.	44,000	29.33	9,680	6.21	36	y
13	Sin, Anna	67,000	44.67	14,740	9.45	54	
14							
15							
16							

That's it for the employee information table. Let's move on to the overhead table:

1. Click Sheet2 to move to a new sheet and rename the sheet as *Overhead*. Then create the first part of the table shown here:

The Overhead sheet

2. M.R. Clean and Anna Sin are officer/employees who do not directly generate income for the company, so we need to include their salaries and benefits in this overhead calculation. You can use the Copy and Paste buttons to copy the entries from C4:F4 of the Employees sheet to C4:F4 of the Overhead sheet, or you can enter them from scratch. If you choose to enter them from scratch, here are the formulas to use in row 4:

C4	=B4/50/30 (with 2-decimal format)
D4	=B4*.22 (with comma 0-decimal format)
E4	=D4/52/30 (with 2-decimal format)
F4	=ROUND(C4+E4,0) (with 0-decimal format)

3. After completing the formulas in row 4, copy them to row 5.

4. Next, enter *Expenses/Hour* in cell E14 and *Total Billable Overhead/Hour* in cell E16. Select both entries and click the Bold and Align Right buttons. The worksheet looks like the one shown on the next page.

Making entries in multiple sheets

When building two or more worksheets with similar layouts, you can select the sheets to form a group and build the layout on all the sheets at the same time. Select nonconsecutive sheets by holding down the Ctrl key and clicking the sheet tabs. Select consecutive sheets by displaying the first sheet, holding down the Shift key, and clicking the tab of the last sheet. The word *Group* appears in the title bar and the selected sheet tabs turn white. You can then build the worksheet. Whatever you do on the displayed sheet is also applied to the other sheets in the group. When you're finished, ungroup the sheets by right-clicking one of the sheet tabs and choosing Ungroup Sheets from the group object menu.

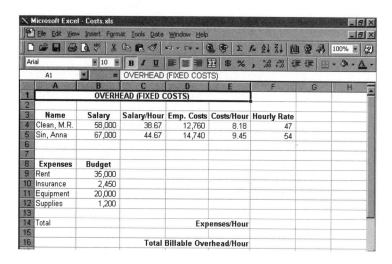

5. Now enter and format these formulas in the designated cells:

B14   =SUM(B9:B13)
F14   =ROUND(B14/52/30,0)
F16   =SUM(F4:F14)

We must bill 30 hours each week at the rate in F16 to cover overhead costs. We cannot bill overhead to a client directly, so we must increase the hourly rate of employees with billable hours by a prorated amount to ensure that overhead is included in project estimates. To calculate the prorated overhead amount, we need to divide the total billable rate per hour in cell F16 by the number of employees who generate income. We can glance at the Employees sheet and know that this number is 8, but what if the company had many employees? We need to reference the cells in the Billable column of the Employees sheet so that Excel can supply this number.

Counting Entries

We can tell Excel to count the number of employees who have a *y* entry in the Billable column of the Employees sheet by using the COUNTA function. This function scans the range specified as its argument and counts the number of nonblank cells in the range. Here's how to use COUNTA in the formula that calculates the overhead allocation:

1. In cell E17 in the Overhead sheet, type *Prorated Overhead/Hour* and click the Enter button.

2. Format the cell by clicking the Bold and Align Right buttons.

3. You want the prorated amount to be in whole dollars, so you need to nest the prorated calculation in a ROUND function. In cell F17, type the following:

=ROUND(F16/COUNTA(

To divide the hourly overhead in cell F16 by the number of employees whose hours are billable, press F3 to display the Paste Name dialog box:

◄─────────────
Pasting a name into
a function

Select Billable and click OK. Type) to close the COUNTA function and then type *,0)* to close the ROUND function. Check that the following function is in the formula bar:

=ROUND(F16/COUNTA(Billable),0)

Then click the Enter button. Excel calculates the formula and enters the value 17 in cell F17, as shown here:

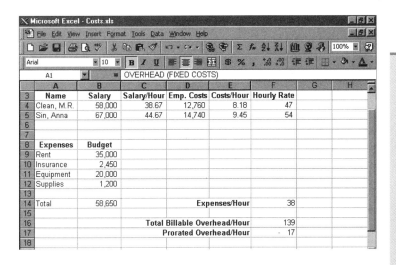

Listing names

Excel keeps track of the ranges to which you have applied a name. You can click a cell in a worksheet, press F3 to display the Paste Name dialog box, and then click the Paste List button to insert a list of range names with their references in the worksheet, starting at the selected cell. If you often assign names (and especially if you use multiple sheets within a workbook), this list can be useful in tracking the locations of the names in the workbook.

4. Assign the name *Over_Rate* to cell F17, and then save the workbook by clicking the Save button.

Creating an Estimate Worksheet

Workbooks as
organizing tools

With the two tables in place, we're ready to create the worksheet for estimating project costs. We'll build this worksheet in a new workbook. First, let's take a few moments to discuss this workbook concept. The purpose of a workbook is to store related sheets of information. For example, if we invoice clients using worksheets, we may want to create a workbook for each client that contains a sheet for each invoice. Or if we don't need to keep an electronic version of every invoice, we could set up a workbook called Invoices that contains a reusable invoice sheet for each client. With a little forethought, we can take advantage of the workbook concept to add a new dimension to our worksheet organization.

In the example we use here, we store the Employees and Overhead sheets in one workbook and then create another workbook for project estimates that uses a new sheet for each project. The employee and overhead information is not stored in the project estimate workbook because this essential business information might be needed in other types of calculations. If we isolate information of this type in its own workbook, we ensure that we don't have to go hunting for it each time we need it.

Now let's open a new workbook and build the basic structure of the project estimate worksheet. Then we'll fill in the formulas necessary for the calculations. Follow these steps:

Flexible formulas

Keep in mind that using names in formulas makes your worksheets much more flexible than using cell references. If the information referenced in a formula moves because of changes you make to a worksheet, Excel adjusts the definition of the name so that the formula continues to access the correct information.

1. Click the New Workbook button on the Standard toolbar and save the new workbook in the My Documents folder as *Estimate*. Then create the top area of the worksheet, as shown on the facing page.

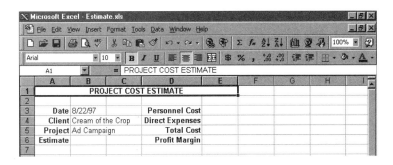

2. Next, enter the headings in row 9 for the table where you'll calculate the personnel costs of the project and enter the employee names and the number of hours you anticipate each will need to work on this project, as shown here:

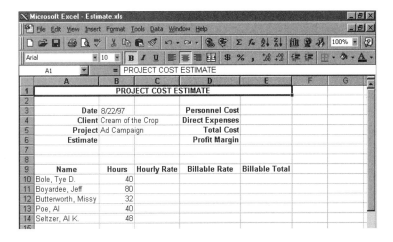

So far, everything has been pretty straightforward and has provided us with nothing more challenging than an opportunity to practice skills we learned in other chapters. Now we need to introduce the Excel function that will enable us to use one of the tables we created earlier to fill in the information needed for this worksheet.

Looking Up Information

Excel has a variety of functions we can use in formulas to look up information in worksheet tables. Among them are VLOOKUP (for vertically oriented tables) and HLOOKUP (for horizontally oriented tables). In this section, we'll show you how to use VLOOKUP. (See the tip on page 137 for

Functions for looking up information

The VLOOKUP function

details about sorting a table before we use Excel to look up information.)

Excel needs three pieces of information to carry out the VLOOKUP function: the entry we want it to look up, the range of the lookup table, and the column number in the table from which the function should copy a value. To search for a value in the lookup table, we supply these three pieces of information in this way:

=VLOOKUP(*lookup_value,table,column_index)*

Excel searches down the leftmost column of the lookup table for the row that contains the value we supply as the first argument. Then, if Excel finds the value, the VLOOKUP function returns the value from the intersection of the same row and the column we supply as the third argument. For example, to look up the hourly rate for Oskar Meyer in the employee information table, we could move to the Employees sheet and enter the following function—say, in cell A17:

=VLOOKUP("Meyer, Oskar",A4:G13,6)

Excel scans the leftmost column of the table in A4:G13—column A—for the lookup value *Meyer, Oskar*. When it finds the value it's looking for in cell A10, it looks across the same row to the sixth column—column F—and copies the value 26 from cell F10 to cell A17.

Let's see how to put the VLOOKUP function to work:

1. In Sheet1 of the Estimate workbook, select cell C10 and click the Paste Function button. With the All option selected, scroll the Function Category list, select VLOOKUP and click OK to display this dialog box:

The Range_lookup argument

By default, the VLOOKUP function searches for the closest match to the lookup_value argument you specify. If you want VLOOKUP to search for an exact match, enter *=FALSE* in the Range_lookup edit box to tell VLOOKUP that a "close enough" search won't meet your needs.

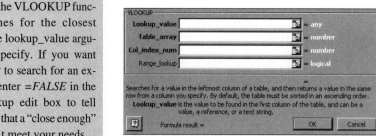

2. With the insertion point in the Lookup_value edit box, click cell A10 on the worksheet. (Use the Collapse and Expand buttons as necesary.) Excel enters A10 in the edit box and displays the contents of the cell next to the edit box.

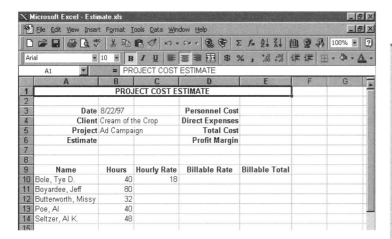

Specifying the lookup value

3. Click the Table_array edit box, choose the Costs workbook from the bottom of the Window menu, and click the Employees tab (even if that sheet is already displayed). Then type *Emp_Rate*. Excel enters a reference to the specified workbook, sheet, and range in the Table_array edit box and establishes a link between the Estimate and Costs workbooks by using the name of the Costs workbook in the formula it is building in the formula bar.

Specifying the lookup table

4. Click the Col_index_num edit box and type *6* to tell Excel to find the answer in the sixth column.

Specifying the lookup column

5. Click OK. Excel immediately looks up the value in cell A10 (Bole, Tye D.) in the lookup table named Emp_Rate on the Employees sheet of the Costs workbook, and enters the corresponding hourly rate in cell C10 of Estimate, as shown here:

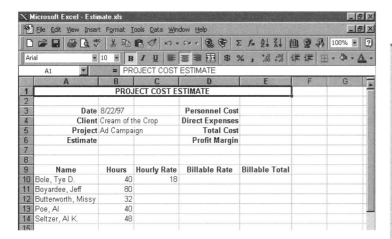

6. Now all you have to do is use AutoFill to copy the formula in cell C10 to C11:C14. Then equivalent formulas will look up the hourly rates for the other people who will be involved in this project.

Easy opening of linked worksheets

When a worksheet contains a reference to a cell on a sheet in a different workbook, Excel asks whether you want to reestablish the link to the cell when you open the worksheet. The linked workbook doesn't have to be open for this retrieval to take place, but if you want, you can easily open it by choosing the Links command from the Edit menu. Excel displays a dialog box listing all workbooks that are referred to by formulas in the active worksheet. Select the workbook you want to open and click the Open Source button.

Completing an Estimate

Well, the hard part is over. A few simple calculations, and we'll be ready to prepare an estimate for Cream of the Crop:

1. In the Estimate workbook, enter the following formula:

   D10 $=C10+Costs!Over\_Rate$

   (You can use the Window menu to choose the Costs workbook. Then click the Overhead tab and type *Over_Rate*. Press Enter to place the formula in the cell and return to the Estimate workbook.)

2. Enter this formula in the indicated cell:

   E10 $=B10*D10$

3. Use AutoFill to copy the formulas to D11:E14.

4. Select C10:E14 and click the Currency Style button on the Formatting toolbar.

5. Press Ctrl+Home to view the results:

6. Now add lines to your table. Select A9:E9, click the arrow to the right of the Borders button, and click the third option in the second row. Then select A14:E14, click the Borders button arrow, and click the second option in the first row.

Now we can calculate total costs in the summary area at the top of the worksheet:

1. Make these entries in the indicated cells:

   E3   =SUM(E10:E14)
   E4   1050
   E5   =E3+E4

2. Use the Currency Style button to format cell E4. (The entry in this cell is an estimate of charges that will be incurred for long-distance phone calls, delivery services, and other expenses attributable directly to the project.) As you can see, this worksheet is almost complete:

Projecting Profit Margin with Iteration

Probably the most difficult part of estimating a project is figuring out the profit margin. We now have a good idea what this project is going to cost. But suppose we need a margin of roughly 35 percent of the estimate total to be sure we make a profit. How do we calculate the actual profit margin when we don't yet know the estimate total, and how do we calculate the estimate total when we don't know the profit margin? We could go in circles forever.

Circular references

Fortunately, we can have Excel go in circles for us. Using the iteration technique, we can force Excel to calculate the profit margin formula over and over until it can give us an answer. Follow the steps on the next page.

1. Select cell E6 in the Estimate workbook, click the Currency Style button, and enter this formula:

   =.35*B6

2. Now select cell B6, click the Currency Style button, and enter this formula:

   =SUM(E5:E6)

   When you enter the second formula, Excel displays a message box stating that it cannot resolve circular references. Here's why: The formula in B6 adds the values in E5 and E6. The formula in E6 multiplies the result of the formula in cell B6 by 35 percent. Excel cannot arrive at a result because when it adds E5 and E6, the formula in E6 must be recalculated; and as soon as Excel recalculates the formula, E6 changes, so E5 and E6 must be added again and so on, forever.

   What is a circular reference?

3. Click OK to close the message box. When Excel displays a Help box explaining circular references, read the information and click the Close button. Your screen looks like this:

The Circular Reference toolbar

You can use the buttons on the Circular Reference toolbar to track down the components of a formula that involves a circular reference. Select a cell reference in the box at the left end of the toolbar and click the Trace Dependents button to see which cells use the selected cell in their formulas. Or click the Trace Precedents button to see which cells are used by the selected cell. The relationships are indicated on the worksheet by tracer arrows. You can remove the arrows by clicking the Remove All Arrows button and then select another cell reference and repeat the tracking process.

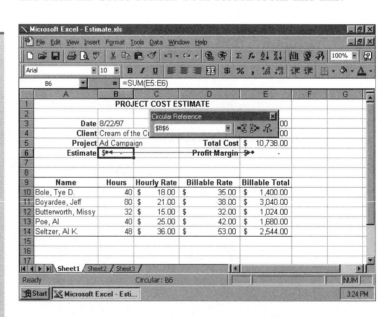

Excel displays a Circular Reference toolbar, and *tracer arrows* identify the cells involved in the formula. The message *Circular: B6* appears in the status bar below the worksheet, telling you that the formula in B6 is the culprit.

Here's how to force Excel to come up with an answer:

1. Close the Circular Reference toolbar.

2. Choose Options from the Tools menu and click the Calculation tab. Excel displays the options shown here:

Turning on Iteration

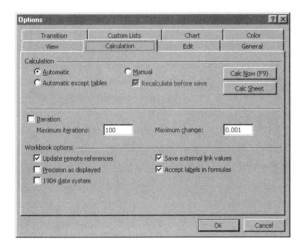

3. Select the Iteration option and then click OK. You return to the worksheet, where Excel quickly recalculates the formulas, finally coming up with the results shown here:

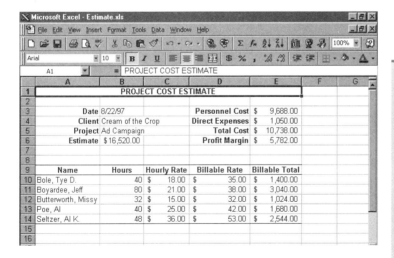

By selecting the Iteration option, you tell Excel to ignore the circular reference and to keep recalculating the formulas,

Types of calculation

By default, Excel immediately calculates a formula when you enter it and also recalculates any of the existing formulas in open worksheets that are affected by the new entry. To tell Excel to calculate open worksheets only when you press the F9 key, choose Options from the Tools menu, click the Calculation tab, and then select the Manual option. You might want to activate this option for large worksheets, where recalculating each formula can take some time.

going in circles. By default, Excel recalculates the formulas 100 times or until the values change by less than .001. The result produced by these settings is not exact, but in this example, the slight inaccuracy is not likely to cause concern. (You can increase the accuracy of the result by changing the Maximum Iterations or Maximum Change setting in the Options dialog box.)

Turning off Iteration →

4. Choose Options from the Tools menu and turn off the Iteration option so that Excel will warn you if you enter a circular reference in another worksheet.

What-If Analysis

The completed project estimate worksheet shows current employee and overhead costs. A number of factors could affect these costs in the future, which would in turn have an impact on the project estimate. In this section, we'll briefly look at three tools for assessing what that impact might be. (A fourth tool, the Solver, deals with multiple variables and constraints and is beyond the scope of this book. Check the online help for information.)

Finding One Unknown Value

Goal Seek →

With Excel, we can use the Goal Seek command on the Tools menu when we know all of a function's arguments except one. As an example, suppose the advertising company is leasing equipment at a cost of $20,000 a year (see cell B11 of the Overhead sheet in the Costs workbook) with a negotiable option to buy that we can exercise in three months. We want to calculate the purchase price that will allow us to buy the equipment without drastically increasing our monthly payments. Follow these steps:

1. Switch to the Costs workbook, activate Sheet3, and name it *Equipment*.

2. Set up the worksheet so that it looks like the one shown at the top of the facing page.

Negative payments

The PMT function takes into account money coming in and going out. If you borrow or buy something on credit, you enter a positive loan amount (or price), and the function displays a negative payment amount—the loan comes in and the payments go out. If you lend money, you enter a negative loan amount, and the function displays a positive payment amount—the loan goes out and the payments come in.

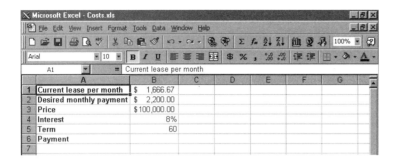

3. Next, enter a PMT function in cell B6 to calculate the loan ◄
   payments, using approximate values. Select cell B6, click the
   Paste Function button, click Financial in the Function Category list, click PMT in the Function Name list, and click OK.

The PMT function

4. In the Rate (for *interest rate*) edit box, click cell B4 and type
   /12 to specify the monthly interest rate.

5. In the Nper (for *number of periodic payments*) edit box, click
   cell B5, and in the Pv (for *present value of the amount
   borrowed*, or the price) edit box, click cell B3. Then click OK.
   Excel calculates the monthly payments for a 60-month (5-
   year) loan of $100,000 at 8% per year.

   Now we'll use Goal Seek to find what price we can afford to
   pay for the equipment if we want our monthly payment to be
   no more than $2,200 per month:

1. With cell B6 selected, choose Goal Seek from the Tools menu
   to display this dialog box, where Excel has entered a reference
   to the selected cell in the Set Cell edit box:

2. Type *2200* in the To Value edit box to tell Excel the maximum
   value allowed in the cell specified in the Set Cell edit box.

3. In the By Changing Cell edit box, click cell B3 to specify that
   this is the value Excel can play with to get the result we want.

Then click OK. When Excel has finished its calculations, it enters the price we are willing to pay for the equipment, $108,500.55, in cell B3 and displays this status box:

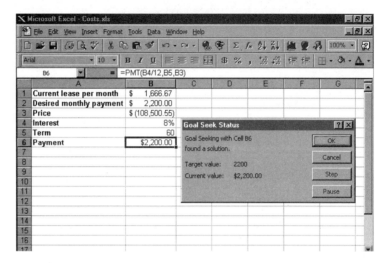

4. Click OK to close the box.

Calculating the Effects of One or Two Variables

Now that we know approximately how much the advertising agency can afford to pay to buy its leased equipment, let's look at the effect that rising or falling interest rates might have on our formula. We could make separate calculations for a range of interest rates, but Excel makes this sort of calculation easy with a tool called *data tables*. Here's how to set up a data table for the advertising agency:

Data tables

The Fill Color button

1. Separate the Goal Seek calculation from the data table by selecting column C, clicking the arrow to the right of the Fill Color button, and selecting any color except white. Then reduce the width of the column.

2. Set up columns E and F of the worksheet to look like the one shown on the facing page (for aesthetic reasons, leave column D blank).

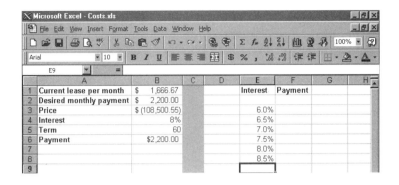

3. Now select cell F2 and enter the following PMT function, which tells Excel to calculate a monthly payment using the annual interest rate in cell E2 (converted to a monthly rate), the number of payments in cell B5, and the price in cell B3:

   =PMT(E2/12,B5,B3)

   Excel uses the formula's arguments to calculate the monthly payment. Because there is no interest rate in cell E2, Excel displays in cell F2 the result when the interest rate is 0% (we wish!). To tell Excel to transfer each of the interest rates in E3:E8 to E2 in turn (in effect, using cell E2 as a kind of scratchpad), we need to define the data table, like this:

4. Select E2:F8 and choose Table from the Data menu to display this dialog box:

5. Because the interest rates are arranged in a column, enter *E2* (the cell used as the PMT function's *rate* argument) in the Column Input Cell edit box and click OK. Excel calculates the PMT function for each of the rates in column E and displays the results in the adjacent cells in column F.

6. Format F2:F8 as currency.

Arrays

If you look at any of the entries in cells F3:F8, you'll see that each result is calculated by the formula {=TABLE(,E2)}. The braces show that Excel is using an array for the calculation. The subject of arrays is beyond the scope of this book, but briefly, an array is a set of values used when calculating formulas that either take multiple values as one of their arguments or produce multiple values as their result.

Now let's quickly see how we would set up the data table to examine the effects of both a varying interest rate and a varying number of payments. Follow these steps:

1. Set up the cells below the first data table to look like this:

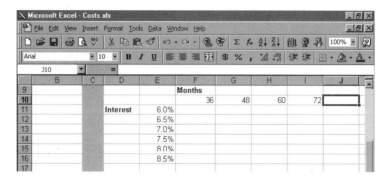

2. Enter the following PMT function in cell E10, the cell at the intersection of the column of rates and the row of monthly payments:

=PMT(D10/12,E9,B3)

Excel uses the specified interest rate (D10/12), number of payments (E9), and price (B3) to calculate the monthly payment. Because there is no interest rate in cell D10 and no number of payments in E9, Excel displays an error message in cell E10. To tell Excel to use the interest rates in E11:E16 and the number of payments in F10:I10, we again need to define the data table.

3. Select E10:I16 and choose Table from the Data menu.

4. In the Row Input Cell edit box, enter *E9* because the numbers of payments are arranged in a row, and in the Column Input Cell edit box, enter *D10* because the interest rates are arranged in a column. Then click OK. Excel calculates the PMT function for each of the rates in column E and the numbers of payments in row 10.

5. Format F11:I16 as currency. The results are displayed on the facing page.

Using a variable range in several formulas

You can use the same variable range to calculate more than one formula. For example, you could enter in cell G2 a second formula that also refers to the empty cell E2, select E2:G8, choose Table from the Data menu, enter a reference to cell E2 in the Column Input Cell edit box, and click OK. The results of the formula in cell F2 will appear in F3:F8, and the results of the formula in cell G2 will appear in G3:G8.

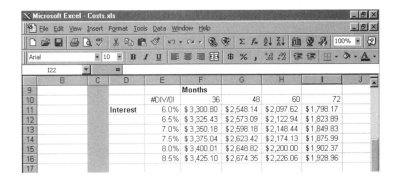

We've gone over data tables very quickly, and you might have trouble understanding them at first. If you want to explore them further, check Excel's online help for more information.

Working with Multiple Scenarios

Suppose the advertising company will be moving into a new facility next year and is looking at two possible locations. How will the move and an anticipated increase in project activity affect overhead costs and, therefore, project costs? We can use Excel's Scenario Manager to create multiple *scenarios* of the expense information so that we can analyze project costs before and after the move.

Scenario Manager

To demonstrate some of the capabilities of Scenario Manager, we'll assign the current nonemployee expenses of the overhead table to a scenario name and create two other scenarios for future nonemployee expenses. Then we'll change the scenarios to see the effect on project costs.

Creating Scenarios

Let's start by designating the expenses range in the Overhead sheet as the changing cells in the scenarios:

1. In the Costs workbook, activate the Overhead sheet, select B9:B12, and choose Scenarios from the Tools menu to display the Scenario Manager dialog box shown on the next page.

Adding the first scenario

2. Click the Add button to display this dialog box:

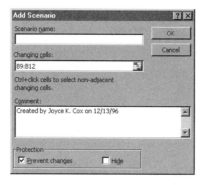

3. Excel has entered the selected range in the Changing Cells edit box. Type *Current Location* in the Scenario Name edit box and click OK to display the Scenario Values dialog box:

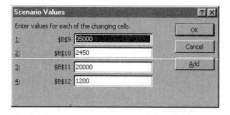

Adding a second scenario

4. The values displayed are those selected in the worksheet. Click Add to keep these values and add the second scenario.

5. Type *First Location* in the Scenario Name edit box and click OK to display the Scenario Values dialog box.

6. Change the values as shown here:

1.	$B$9	*43000*
2.	$B$10	*3500*
3.	$B$11	*21000*
4.	$B$12	*2200*

Then click Add again to keep these numbers and add the third scenario.   ← Adding a third scenario

7. Type *Second Location* in the Scenario Name edit box and click OK.

8. Change the values as shown here:

1.	$B$9	*48000*
2.	$B$10	*4500*
3.	$B$11	*27500*
4.	$B$12	*4200*

Then click OK to return to the Scenario Manager dialog box, which now looks like this:

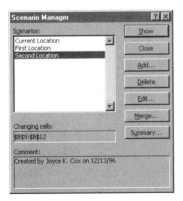

9. Click Close to return to the workbook.

Changing Scenarios

By changing scenarios, we can display different versions of a worksheet to see the results of various conditions or assumptions. In the project estimate worksheet, we can use the scenarios we've created to show the effect of future overhead costs on project costs and profit margin.

Merging scenarios

You can create a worksheet with a scenario and send copies to colleagues to input their scenario values. When they return their copies, you can click the Merge button in the Scenario Manager dialog box, select their worksheets, and merge them into Scenario Manager, where you can view and edit their scenarios or use them in summary reports.

To make it easier to access the scenarios and see their effects, we'll display the Costs and Estimate workbooks side by side. Follow the steps below to set up the screen:

1. Choose Arrange from the Window menu and click OK to accept the default Tiled option.

2. Scroll columns D and E into view in the Estimate window.

We are now ready to run the scenarios. Here's how:

Selecting a scenario

1. Activate the Costs workbook, choose Scenarios from the Tools menu, select First Location in the Scenarios box, click Show, and click Close. The expense cells change based on the values we defined for the First Location scenario, and Excel recalculates both workbooks, as shown below. (You may have to scroll the appropriate areas into view.)

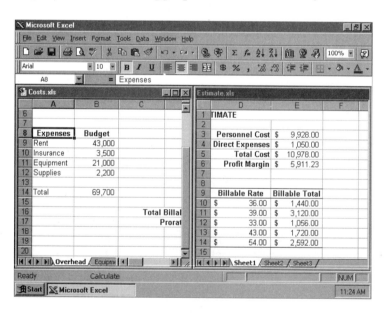

2. Display the Scenario Manager dialog box again, select Second Location from the Scenarios box, and click Show and then Close to produce these results:

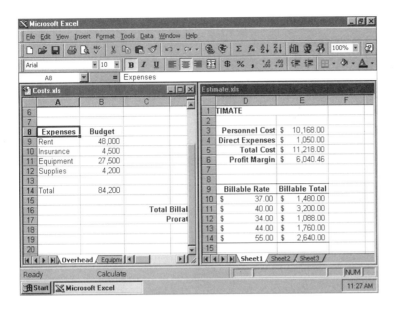

3. Return the expense cells to their original values by selecting Current Location from the Scenarios box in the Scenario Manager dialog box. Then maximize the Costs window.

Creating Scenario Reports

Now that we have completed the building of the scenarios, let's use Scenario Manager to print a report. The Scenario Summary report displays the values of all the scenarios and their effects on the result cells. In this example, the result cell is the Prorated Overhead/Hour amount in cell F17 in the Overhead sheet of the Costs workbook. It shows the amount of increase in the hourly rate of employees needed to ensure that the increase in overhead is taken into account in project estimates. Here's how to generate a report:

The Scenario Summary

1. Choose Scenarios from the Tools menu to display the Scenario Manager dialog box.

2. Click the Summary button, which displays the dialog box shown here:

By default, Scenario Manager has selected the Scenario Summary option in the Report Type section and entered a reference to F17 in the Result Cells edit box.

3. Click OK. Scenario Manager creates a new sheet named Scenario Summary between the Employees and Overhead sheets in the Costs workbook and builds the report.

4. Scroll column G into view so that you can view the report shown here:

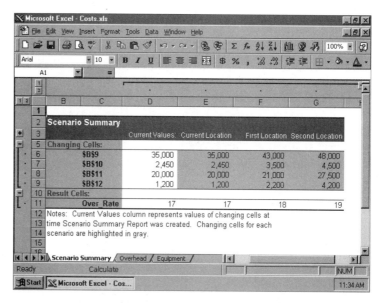

As you can see, Scenario Manager displays the report in outline format so that you can easily hide or unhide rows and columns. (See the tip on page 80 for more information about outlining worksheets.)

5. If you want a printed copy of the report, click the Print button. Then save and close both workbooks.

We now have a completed project estimate that takes into account the overhead costs as well as the direct costs associated with the advertising project. We also have a means of assessing the impact of varying overhead costs, and we can easily set up scenarios to examine the effects of other changes, such as salary increases.

As we said at the beginning of the chapter, we can adapt this set of worksheets in many ways to help us quickly assemble bids. We can also use versions of these worksheets for such tasks as comparing the cost of doing projects in-house with estimates that we receive from vendors. And once we have set up a lookup table such as the employee information table, we can link it to worksheets that perform a variety of other personnel-related calculations.

Index

Quick Course®
books—first-class training at
economy prices!

"...perfect to help groups of new users become productive quickly."
—PC Magazine

Perfect for educators and trainers, Quick Course® books offer streamlined instruction for the new user in the form of no-nonsense, to-the-point tutorials and learning exercises. The core of each book is a logical sequence of straightforward, easy-to-follow instructions for building useful business documents—the same documents people create and use on the job.

Microsoft Office 97

U.S.A.	$24.99
U.K.	£22.99
Canada	$34.99
ISBN	1-57231-726-4

Microsoft Windows 95

U.S.A.	$14.99
U.K.	£13.99
Canada	$20.99
ISBN	1-57231-727-2

Microsoft Word 97

U.S.A.	$14.99
U.K.	£13.99
Canada	$20.99
ISBN	1-57231-725-6

Microsoft Excel 97

U.S.A.	$14.99
U.K.	£13.99
Canada	$20.99
ISBN	1-57231-723-X

Microsoft Access 97

U.S.A.	$14.99
U.K.	£13.99
Canada	$20.99
ISBN	1-57231-722-1

Microsoft PowerPoint 97

U.S.A.	$14.99
U.K.	£13.99
Canada	$20.99
ISBN	1-57231-724-8

Microsoft® Press

Things are looking up!

Here's the remarkable, *visual* way to quickly find answers about Microsoft applications and operating systems. Microsoft Press® *At a Glance* books let you focus on particular tasks and show you with clear, numbered steps the easiest way to get them done right now.

Microsoft® Excel 97 At a Glance
Perspection, Inc.
U.S.A. $16.95   ($22.95 Canada)
ISBN 1-57231-367-6

Microsoft® Word 97 At a Glance
Jerry Joyce and Marianne Moon
U.S.A. $16.95   ($22.95 Canada)
ISBN 1-57231-366-8

Microsoft® PowerPoint® 97 At a Glance
Perspection, Inc.
U.S.A. $16.95   ($22.95 Canada)
ISBN 1-57231-368-4

Microsoft® Access 97 At a Glance
Perspection, Inc.
U.S.A. $16.95   ($22.95 Canada)
ISBN 1-57231-369-2

Microsoft® Office 97 At a Glance
Perspection, Inc.
U.S.A. $16.95   ($22.95 Canada)
ISBN 1-57231-365-X

Microsoft® Windows® 95 At a Glance
Jerry Joyce and Marianne Moon
U.S.A. $16.95   ($22.95 Canada)
ISBN 1-57231-370-6

Microsoft Press® products are available worldwide wherever quality computer books are sold. For more information, contact your book or computer retailer, software reseller, or local Microsoft Sales Office, or visit our Web site at mspress.microsoft.com. To locate your nearest source for Microsoft Press products, or to order directly, call 1-800-MSPRESS in the U.S. (in Canada, call 1-800-268-2222).

Prices and availability dates are subject to change.

Microsoft Press